Effective STUdy STRATEGiES for Every Classroom

Grades 7–12

Also from the Boys Town Press

The Well-Managed Classroom, 2nd Edition
Tools for Teaching Social Skills in School
Teaching Social Skills to Youth, 2nd Edition
No Room for Bullies
The 100-Yard Classroom
Safe and Effective Secondary Schools
Changing Children's Behavior by Changing the People,
    Places, and Activities in Their Lives
Treating Youth with DSM-IV Disorders
Common Sense Parenting® DVDs:
    Building Relationships
    Teaching Children Self-Control
    Correcting Misbehavior
    Preventing Problem Behavior

Getting Along with Others
Common Sense Parenting®
Common Sense Parenting of Toddlers and Preschoolers
Common Sense Parenting Learn-at-Home DVD Kit
There Are No Simple Rules for Dating My Daughter
Who's Raising Your Child?
Time to Enrich Before and After School Activity Kit
Angry Kids, Frustrated Parents
Dealing with Your Kids' 7 Biggest Troubles
Unmasking Sexual Con Games
Good Night, Sweet Dreams, I Love You: Now Get into Bed and Go to Sleep
Parenting to Build Character in Your Teen
Practical Tools for Foster Parents
Skills for Families, Skills for Life
Getting Along with Others

For Teens

Guys, Let's Keep It Real
Little Sisters, Listen Up
Boundaries: A Guide for Teens
A Good Friend
Who's in the Mirror?
What's Right for Me?

For a free Boys Town Press catalog, call 1-800-282-6657.
www.boystownpress.org

Boys Town National Hotline 1-800-448-3000
Parents and kids can call toll-free, anytime, with any problem.

Effective STUdy STRATEGiES for Every Classroom

Grades 7–12

29 lesson plans for teaching note-taking, summarizing, researching and test-taking skills

Jeanne R. Mach, Rebecca Lash-Rabick, M.Ed., Carol Meysenburg Johnson, M.S., Jacqueline Bode Frevert, M.S., Suzann Morin-Steffen, M.S., and Jennifer Buth Bell, M.S. Ed.Ad.

BOYS TOWN Press ℠

Boys Town, Nebraska

Effective Study Strategies for Every Classroom

Published by the Boys Town Press
Father Flanagan's Boys' Home
Boys Town, NE 68010

Copyright © 2008, Father Flanagan's Boys' Home
ISBN-10: 1-889322-94-6
ISBN-13: 978-1-889332-94-9

15 14 13 12 11 10 9 8 7 6 5 4 3 2 1

Table of Contents

Section 3

Section 4

Study Skills for Students

These four students each faced a different academic task. Because they were so ill-prepared, failure was inevitable...

PREPARATION

❶ Stuart has a quiz over Chapter 2 of *The Hobbit*. His English teacher said students could use one note card during the quiz. Stuart spends the night before the quiz writing, almost verbatim and in tiny print, as much of the chapter as he can squeeze on his note card.

❷ Janelle's in-class history assignment is to write a brief summary of the 1963 March on Washington. Janelle decides to copy all of the notes she took during the lecture and turn that in as her summary.

❸ Reggie's geography assignment is to write a two-page report about Thailand. He uses the Web site "Wikipedia" as his sole information source.

❹ Tori is nervous about her afternoon algebra exam. She stresses out any time she has to take a test. On this day, she decides to skip lunch because her nerves have her stomach in knots. Better to go into the exam room on an empty stomach than one full and queasy, she thinks.

PERFORMANCE

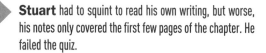

Stuart had to squint to read his own writing, but worse, his notes only covered the first few pages of the chapter. He failed the quiz.

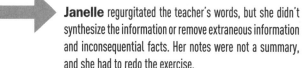

Janelle regurgitated the teacher's words, but she didn't synthesize the information or remove extraneous information and inconsequential facts. Her notes were not a summary, and she had to redo the exercise.

Reggie's Thailand report included the phrase "[citation needed]." The term, which appears often on some Wikipedia entries, was a dead giveaway that he had copied word-for-word information from the Web site. He earned a zero on the assignment and a detention for plagiarism.

Tori was so hungry during the exam, her stomach growled repeatedly. She couldn't concentrate on the questions. Embarrassed, she worried more about keeping her stomach from rumbling than finishing the formulas. Class ended before she answered all of the questions.

What went wrong for these students? One could argue that Stuart was sloppy. Janelle was confused. Reggie was lazy. And Tori was sick. And there would be some truth in such assumptions. But for the vast majority of students who experience similar failings, the problem isn't a lack of desire or poor health. It's a more fundamental problem: A basic lack of study skills. Too many students simply have not learned how to learn.

The reasons why students lack proper study skills vary. Some young people simply have never been taught how to take notes, use an encyclopedia or online research tools, review appropriate material, identify important facts and information, prepare for tests, or use other critical strategies that support academic achievement. Many others simply lack experience using study skills or have misguided notions about how to succeed and who succeeds in the classroom. For example, we know students who believe that if they spend 30 minutes studying for an exam or working on an assignment, they will automatically be successful. To them, success is determined by an arbitrary length of time rather than the quality or effectiveness of that study time.

Then of course, there are a few students who believe good grades are not based on merit but on popularity. They have the self-defeating belief that teachers award the best grades to the students they like the most. So when they earn a poor grade, the fault lies with a teacher who is "out to get them," not with their own lack of preparation or performance. (As an educator, it's important that you evaluate your relationships with students so such attitudes don't become accepted as fact and an excuse for failure. For effective strategies on reaching out and connecting with students and building a sense of trust and community in your classroom, we recommend reading *The Well-Managed Classroom, 2nd Ed.,* another Boys Town Press publication.)

When discussing study skills, teachers often lament the lack of formal instruction offered to students in this area or the limited practical experience their students have in applying study strategies in their everyday activities. But what's even more disheartening to some are the students who were taught study skills yet continue to struggle. Why is this? In our experience, many of these students may have poor reading skills, or they really haven't mastered good study habits.

Students who struggle with the printed word are at a severe disadvantage in the classroom. The ability to decode words, read sentences, and comprehend information is essential for learning. Imagine for a moment that you are a student who struggles to decode words. You have to focus so much energy on pronouncing words and phrases in the text, you can't concentrate on anything else. What is an exam question really asking you? What is the meaning of a paragraph? What is the main idea in the text? It's nearly impossible to know the answers to such questions if you've spent several minutes simply trying to decode a single word.

Here's another way to think about what some of your students might be experiencing:

Say, for example, a student's brain is made up of 10 apples that he or she can work with at any given time. Because the student struggles with decoding, eight apples are dedicated to pronouncing individual words and phrases. That leaves two apples for comprehension. But reading requires equal amounts of decoding and comprehension at all times. As a result, the student's ability to comprehend the material is compromised.[1]

Given the challenges that confront poor readers, it may be necessary for you to assess the reading skills of students before introducing the study strategies outlined in this manual. Students will need basic comprehension skills in order to get the most benefit from the lesson plans. There are many excellent reading intervention programs for adolescents, including Reading Is FAME® from Boys Town, that can reverse reading failure in students. If you are working with youth who have significant reading deficiencies, you may need to adjust and adapt the lessons accordingly.

Comprehension problems, however, are not limited to poor readers or students labeled "academically challenged." A-level students can struggle, too. In one study of high-achieving ninth-graders, a surprising number admitted that they FREQUENTLY experience confusion after reading several pages of text. Their inability to comprehend what they just read is magnified by the fact that they do not regularly or effectively use study skills. Poor note taking, last-minute cramming for exams, and failing to review and organize material were all problem areas for these honors students.[2]

Regardless of how academically gifted students may be, many have a limited understanding and repertoire of good study habits. This helps to explain why even students who were taught study skills in the past sometimes have trouble accessing their prior knowledge and implementing the strategies effectively and efficiently. As you assess the study skills that your students lack or need to improve, ask yourself these questions:

- Do my students understand or know what study skills are?

- Do my students have trouble generalizing study skills to different contexts and subject areas?

- Do my students rely on a limited number of strategies and employ them poorly?

- Do some of my students read below grade level, and if so, which study skills can provide them the most immediate benefit?

Today's classrooms are filled with students who are as cognitively different as they are culturally diverse. The better you can understand the reasons why your students' struggle with study skills, the more targeted and successful your instructional approach will be. The lesson plans contained in these pages are designed to help you empower all of your students to achieve their academic goals.

As classroom teachers, reading specialists, and education consultants with more than 100 combined years of instructional and administrative experience, we see firsthand what students are capable of achieving when they learn how to learn. We also know the struggles young people endure when they lack such ability. Study skills are often a determining factor in academic achievement. Research shows that students who possess a broad range of study skills outperform (in terms of grade point, test scores, and other performance measures) those who rely on a single skill. And "superior academic performance" is associated with students who know how to take notes, summarize and synthesize information, identify main ideas, and understand which study strategies are most appropriate for any given task.[3]

We all want students to excel in and outside of the classroom. By teaching essential study strategies, we can make learning easier for students and give them the confidence and ability to consistently achieve their academic goals.

How to Use This Book

We've seen and used many study skills books. To our surprise and disappointment, most were not written by teachers who worked in the trenches (which may explain why some of the suggestions and strategies seemed so impractical). Other books focused on only one or two skill areas. This meant we had to search for and sort through multiple books, which wasn't very efficient. Those experiences motivated us to create a more practical guide to study skills instruction – one that is teacher-tested, user-friendly, and broad-based, with enjoyable learning activities.

In developing the content, we incorporated the best-known, most effective, and most practical study skills into simple, easy-to-use lesson plans. Our decision about which study strategies to include involved the following considerations:

- Can the skill be generalized to every subject?

- Is it easy to teach and learn?

- Can it be practiced by individual students and in groups?

- Does it help further students' knowledge and mastery of the subject matter being taught?

- Is it a skill a student can use throughout his or her school career and beyond?

Based on these criteria, our personal classroom experience, and the consultation work we've done with school systems across the country, it was clear that four specific types of study skills offered the greatest potential for positive change and academic success – **note taking, summarizing, researching,** and **test taking.**

These four study skills are ones that every student should know and be able to use. In their popular book, *Classroom Instruction that Works* (2001), authors Marzano, Pickering, and Pollack identified nine types of instructional strategies shown to have a "strong effect on student achievement."[4] Included among the nine strategies are several associated with study skills – summarizing and note taking, identifying similarities and differences, and organizing information. These strategies, among many others, are the focus of the lesson plans in this manual.

To make this book practical, inclusive, and focused on best practices, we wrote whole lesson plans that, hopefully, will make you feel more competent and confident to teach study skills. The lessons incorporate two key concepts of effective teaching:

- 100-percent active participation by students

- Continuous checking for understanding by the teacher

GROW Input Method

The lesson plans are designed to be taught using the **GROW Input** method of direct instruction. This strategy, as outlined in these lessons, reflects the work of Madeline Hunter as well as the contributions of other educators and educational agencies, including Suzann Morin-Steffen, the Utah Learning Resource Center, and the Loess Hills (Iowa) Area Education Agency 13.

GROW Input is an instructional strategy that encourages you to continually engage students by asking questions and seeking feedback. As you teach the lessons, ask questions that relate to both academics and comprehension (for example, do they understand what I'm asking them to do in a lesson?). You may need to do some pre-teaching prior to the lessons, reminding students that they should think of answers to every question asked because they may be called on at any time. When students answer questions correctly, praise them. If a student doesn't know an answer, provide prompts until he or she can answer correctly. This approach shows you will stick with students rather than "abandon" them if they answer incorrectly or respond with "I don't know." As an instructional method, **GROW Input** fosters active participation from all students, helps them maintain focus, and ensures that they are "with" you and "get" it.

The steps or stages of the **GROW Input** method are built into each lesson's introduction. You start by **G**aining students' attention, then **R**eview key details (if applicable) from a previous lesson, state the lesson's **O**bjective, and explain **W**hy the objective or skill has value for the students. After this introduction, you start teaching the actual lesson (the **Input**). We've provided directions and talking points to guide your instruction, including how and when to use the support materials. (Each lesson plan has pages with information and illustrations that are labeled "Overhead." You can convert these pages into transparencies or any other format that corresponds with the available technology.) Prompts are included as reminders to continually engage students by asking for feedback and checking for understanding. At the end of each lesson are suggestions on how to summarize the lesson and move on to other follow-up activities or a new lesson. For added convenience, the enclosed CD-ROM allows you to easily reproduce the lessons, support materials, and worksheets as needed.

We've broken the content into four sections that build on each other. Section 1 emphasizes note taking, including a lesson on the Cornell Method. If students are poor note takers, it will be far more difficult for them to develop or master any other study strategies. Section 2 complements note taking with lessons designed to strengthen students' abilities to summarize information. With note taking and summarizing as a foundation, Section 3 adds another essential strategy – using research tools (encyclopedias, almanacs, and the Internet). All of these lessons lead naturally into the final section of the book, test taking. Lesson plans on overcoming anxiety and distinguishing between different types of exam questions are included.

The goal of this manual is to provide a fresh perspective and a more practical approach to study skills instruction. We know your professional experience has given you valuable insights into effective teaching strategies and methods. Hopefully, this book will complement your efforts to improve the study skills of all your students.

About the Authors

Jeanne R. Mach has taught courses in physics, chemistry, human anatomy, physiology, and life and physical sciences in Kansas and Nebraska schools. She served on numerous committees for the Westside Community Schools (Omaha, NE) that promoted reading improvement and effective instruction. Mach earned her bachelor's degree from Baker University (Kansas) and is currently a Reading Is FAME instructor at Boys Town High School.

Rebecca Lash-Rabick is a teacher in the Bellevue (NE) Public Schools. She has taught English, French, and reading in both public and private high schools. Lash-Rabick is a former program coordinator for the Boys Town Reading Is FAME program. She has written several articles for professional publications and is a sought-after lecturer at regional and national conferences on reading. Lash-Rabick earned a bachelor's degree from the University of Iowa and a master's degree from the University of Missouri.

Carol Meysenburg Johnson has more than 20 years of classroom experience. She has taught remedial reading, math, and computer technology courses. Johnson currently is a Reading Is FAME coordinator for Boys Town schools. She earned her master's degree in behavior disorders from the University of Nebraska at Omaha.

Jacqueline Bode Frevert has been a teacher, counselor, coach, and administrator at the high school and college level. She has presented numerous workshops on issues ranging from classroom management to active classroom participation. Frevert earned a bachelor's degree from Wayne State College (Nebraska) and a master's degree from the University of Nebraska at Omaha.

Suzann Morin-Steffen is a former senior team leader for the Boys Town Reading Center, where she coordinated the dissemination of Reading Is FAME. She has served as a special education consultant for the state of Iowa, directed a high school for at-risk students, and been published in the journal, *Teaching Exceptional Children*. Morin-Steffen has taught students at every grade level, including adults in community college reading classes. She has a bachelor's degree from the University of Montana and a master's degree from the University of Nebraska at Omaha.

Jennifer Buth Bell is the manager of the Boys Town Reading Center. She has a broad range of educational experience, including work as a classroom teacher, coach, professional development specialist, curriculum developer, online instructor, and administrator. As an education consultant, she worked with hundreds of schools and educational

programs nationwide. Buth Bell earned a bachelor's degree in elementary education from Concordia College (Minnesota), a master's degree in education administration from the University of Nebraska at Omaha, and is currently working toward a second master's degree in reading.

[1] Laberge, D., & Samuels, S.J. (1974). Toward a theory of automatic information processing in reading. **Cognitive Psychology,** 6, 293-323.

[2] Stanley, B., Slate, J.R., & Jones, C.H. (1999). Study behaviors of college preparatory and honors students in the ninth grade. **The High School Journal,** 82, 165-171.

[3] Purdie, N., & Hattie, J. (1999). The relationship between study skills and learning outcomes: A meta-analysis. **Australian Journal of Education,** 43 (1), 72-86.

[4] Marzano, R.J., Pickering, D.J., & Pollock, J.E. (2001). **Classroom instruction that works.** Alexandria, VA: Association for Supervision and Curriculum Development.

Note-Taking Strategies

s it hard to take notes? For many students, the answer is a resounding yes. It's estimated that students taking notes during a lecture will only capture 20 to 40 percent of the main ideas.[1] This statistic is particularly troubling when you consider that lectures are a primary instructional approach, especially in secondary classrooms.

Students who take incomplete notes often are at risk for underperforming on exams and quizzes. Several research studies reveal that students who take more comprehensive notes and review them prior to exams score better than peers who take minimal notes.[2] While taking more notes is better than taking less, students who go too far and copy everything they read and hear can also sabotage their study efforts. Verbatim notes (as Stuart painfully demonstrated in our Introduction) are ineffective because such an approach sacrifices a student's ability to synthesize and analyze information.[3]

To help find the right balance, the following lesson plans teach students how to discern key words, main ideas, and relevant facts from the irrelevant, insignificant, and immaterial. The lessons are divided into two groups: general note taking and note-taking formats.

The general note-taking lessons cover these skills: using signal words, following basic guidelines, and using abbreviations and symbols. The lessons on formatting introduce these strategies: the Five W's and How method, the Cornell Method, T-charts, concept maps, the four-square method, and the vocabulary tri-fold method.

At the end of Section 1, you'll find 14 short articles. Some of these reading passages are integrated into specific lessons. However, you can mix and match the articles to accommodate your individual needs.

---

[1] Kiewra, K.A. (2002). How classroom teachers can help students learn and teach them how to learn. **Theory Into Practice,** 4 (2), 71-80.

[2] Sweeney, W.J., Ehrhardt, A.M., Gardner III, R., Jones, L., Greenfield, R., & Fribley, S. (1999). Using guided notes with academically at-risk high school students during a remedial summer social studies class. **Psychology in the Schools,** 36 (4), 305-318.

[3] Marzano, R.J., Pickering, D.J., & Pollock, J.E. (2001). **Classroom instruction that works.** Alexandria, VA: Association for Supervision and Curriculum Development.

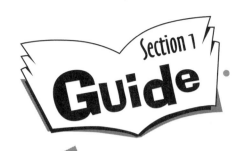

General Note-Taking Lessons

Note-Taking Formats

Articles

Using Signal Words

OBJECTIVE

Students will be able to identify "signal words" – presentation cues, superlatives, definitions, supporting details, opposing details, illustrations, absolutes, and conclusions – and use them to find main ideas and supporting details in printed text.

MATERIALS

Overhead or LCD projector

Overheads
Presentation Cues
Superlatives
Definitions
Supporting Details
Opposing Details
Illustrations
Absolutes
Conclusions

Worksheet (one per student)
Identifying Signal Words

Article (one per student)
Chinese Characters, pg. 92

Answer Key Overhead
Chinese Characters

APPROXIMATE TIME

30 minutes or
three 10-minute mini-lessons

Introduction

- **G**ain students' attention.
- **R**eview key details from the most recent lesson (if applicable).
- Clearly state the **O**bjective of the lesson:
  - □ "Today's lesson is about how signal words are used to indicate main ideas and supporting details. Signal words are terms or expressions that authors use to guide readers to important information. You are going to read an article, identify signal words, and determine what the main ideas and supporting details are."
- Explain **W**hy students should learn the information.
  - □ Explain to students that when they learn how to recognize signal words in reading material, they will know how to find information that the author considers important. Being able to identify main ideas and key details makes note taking much easier.
  - □ Ask students, "How many of you have driven through, or ridden with someone who has driven through, a yellow traffic signal?" Wait for responses, then follow up by asking students to think about what a yellow traffic light means. Call on someone to answer.
  - □ Explain to students that just as a yellow traffic light tells drivers to slow down and pay attention, writers use words to signal readers to be attentive because important information is being presented. Tell your students that they are going to practice how to identify those signal words in today's lesson.

Teacher Input/Modeling

- Use direct instruction to introduce the different categories of signal words and give examples of how they are used.

☐ Using the overheads, go through the eight types of signal words. Have students follow along by filling in the blanks on their Identifying Signal Words worksheet (distributed earlier). Periodically ask questions to ensure comprehension and participation. After each example, have students identify the signal words used in the sentence. Walk around and check students' worksheets for accuracy. Provide the correct answers by underlining or circling the signal words on the overhead. Before you instruct students to find signal words on their own, using the *Chinese Characters* article (page 92), do a quick review and have students give examples of different types of signal words.

Guided/Independent Practice

■ Hand out copies of the *Chinese Characters* article and instruct students to underline, highlight, or circle any signal words they find, and then label what category or type of signal it is.

Closure/Review

■ Use the Answer Key overhead to review students' *Chinese Characters* assignment.

■ Discuss the signal words used in the article and what important information each word signaled.

■ Summarize the lesson by reminding students that their ability to recognize signal words will make it easier for them to locate and identify important facts and key details.

Connection/Extension

■ To extend the lesson, have students identify signal words in other reading material, using whatever note-taking format you want them to practice.

■ This lesson also complements writing exercises, including how to use transition words or phrases in written summaries. Most of the signal words introduced in this lesson also function as transition words that students can use in their writing assignments.

TYPE OF SIGNAL
Presentation Cues

Watch for different print styles to indicate important information:

Words in bold print

Words in italics

WORDS IN ALL CAPS

Topics and subtopics printed larger or in **different colors** or different fonts

<u>Words underlined</u>

EXAMPLE

The structure of the human brain:

The brain looks like a large gray mushroom with many folds, called <u>convolutions.</u> The brain is made up of three main parts: the *cerebrum,* the *cerebellum,* and the *medulla oblongata.*

TYPE OF SIGNAL
Superlatives

Superlatives are words that describe details as unique and worthy of remembering.

These facts are "super important" or superlatives.

These details are often included on tests.

They usually will include "most" words or "-est" words.

EXAMPLES

The **most** important thing to remember when driving is to keep your eyes on the road.

The **tallest** building in the world is the Taipei Financial Center, a 101-story tower that stands more than 1,600-feet high.

Definitions

Definitions are phrases that often appear before or after:

Highlighted words

Boldfaced words

Italicized words

<u>**Underlined**</u> words

Punctuation, such as a comma, hyphen, or colon

EXAMPLES

Comets, frozen masses of dust and gas revolving around the sun in an orbit, are often the subject of movies, television programs, and newspaper articles.

The spinal cord is connected to the brain by the **medulla oblongata**.

TYPE OF SIGNAL
Supporting Details

Information that follows these signal words help to support or expand the ideas that came before them. Several examples include:

More

Another

Additionally

And

Also

Likewise

Furthermore

Moreover

Lists

EXAMPLES

There are three main reasons why my sister likes her job as a teacher: 1) She enjoys working with children, 2) she loves helping students discover and learn new things, and 3) she likes having summer vacation.

One way people travel is by airplane. Another way is by bus. Additionally, some people like to travel by driving their own car.

TYPE OF SIGNAL
Opposing Details

Information that follows these signal words reverse or oppose the ideas that came before them. Several examples of opposing details include:

Although

Contrary

However

But

Yet

Otherwise

Nevertheless

Not

Despite

EXAMPLES

Solar energy has no pollution; it is a very clean source of energy. However, solar energy is expensive to use because you must install your own solar panels.

Most people in the Midwest use their own transportation instead of public transportation, despite the rising cost of fuel and the pollution.

Illustrations

Illustrations are words used to signal examples that expand or clarify information:

For example

For instance

An illustration of this

EXAMPLES

There are many reasons why people should consider carpooling. For example, look at the money you can save.

It's dangerous to talk on your cell phone while you are driving. An illustration of this is the car accident that was on the news.

TYPE OF SIGNAL
Absolutes

Absolutes are words that signal the information is pointing out something rare. This kind of information is often found on true/false tests. Examples include:

Always

All

Everyone

No one

Never

None

EXAMPLES

Gravity is always present on earth.

When the space shuttle Challenger exploded, it killed all seven crewmembers, shocked the nation, started a NASA investigation, and led to many changes in the space program.

Conclusions

Conclusions are words that signal the idea is an overall concept or result. Examples include:

In summary

In conclusion

Thus

Because

Therefore

As a result

EXAMPLES

As a result of his greed, the game show contestant went home with only one cent.

Many people own cell phones now that didn't own them five years ago. As a result, long distance telephone companies are offering savings to try to lure back customers.

Identifying Signal Words

Name: _____ Date: _____

Directions: Complete the worksheet by filling in information provided on the overhead. In each example, circle the signal word(s) used.

TYPE OF SIGNAL: _____

Watch for different print styles to indicate important information:

_____

_____

_____

_____

EXAMPLE:

The structure of the human brain:

The brain looks like a large gray mushroom with many folds, called <u>convolutions</u>. The brain is made up of three main parts: the *cerebrum*, the *cerebellum*, and the *medulla oblongata*.

_____

TYPE OF SIGNAL: _____

Superlatives are words that describe details as unique and worthy of remembering.

_____

_____

_____

_____

EXAMPLES:

The most important thing to remember when driving is to keep your eyes on the road.

The tallest building in the world is the Taipei Financial Center, a 101-story tower that stands more than 1,600-feet high.

TYPE OF SIGNAL: _____

Definitions are phrases that often appear before or after:

_____

_____

_____

_____

EXAMPLES:

Comets, frozen masses of dust and gas revolving around the sun in an orbit, are often the subject of movies, television programs, and newspaper articles.

The spinal cord is connected to the brain by the **medulla oblongata**.

TYPE OF SIGNAL: _____

Information that follows these signal words help to support or expand the ideas that came before them. Several examples include:

_____

_____

_____

_____

EXAMPLES:

There are three main reasons why my sister likes her job as a teacher: 1) She enjoys working with children, 2) she loves helping students discover and learn new things, and 3) she likes having summer vacation.

One way people travel is by airplane. Another way is by bus. Additionally, some people like to travel by driving their own car.

TYPE OF SIGNAL: _____

Information that follows these signal words reverse or oppose the ideas that came before them. Several examples of opposing details include:

_____

_____

_____

_____

EXAMPLES:

Solar energy has no pollution; it is a very clean source of energy. However, solar energy is expensive to use because you must install your own solar panels.

Most people in the Midwest use their own transportation instead of public transportation, despite the rising cost of fuel and the pollution.

TYPE OF SIGNAL: _____

Illustrations are words used to signal examples that expand or clarify information:

_____

_____

_____

_____

EXAMPLES:

There are many reasons why people should consider car pooling. For example, look at the money you can save.

It's dangerous to talk on your cell phone while you are driving. An illustration of this is the car accident that was on the news.

TYPE OF SIGNAL: _____

Absolutes are words that signal the information is pointing out something rare.
This kind of information is often found on true/false tests. Examples include:

_____

_____

_____

_____

EXAMPLES:

Gravity is always present on earth.

When the space shuttle Challenger exploded, it killed all seven crewmembers,
shocked the nation, started a NASA investigation, and led to many changes in the
space program.

TYPE OF SIGNAL: _____

Conclusions are words that signal the idea is an overall concept or result. Examples include:

_____

_____

_____

_____

EXAMPLES:

As a result of his greed, the game show contestant went home with only one cent.

Many people own cell phones now that didn't own them five years ago. As a result, long
distance telephone companies are offering savings to try to lure back customers.

22

Chinese Characters

Below is a list of the signal words found in the *Chinese Characters* article, including their category or type.

Superlatives: most, oldest

Supporting details: also

Opposing details: unlike, however, regardless

Illustrations: such as

Conclusions: in other words

Following Note-Taking Guidelines

OBJECTIVE

Students will be able to follow basic note-taking guidelines and practice their note-taking skills while listening to a lecture.

MATERIALS

Overhead or LCD projector

Overhead
Note-Taking Guidelines

APPROXIMATE TIME

10 minutes

Introduction

- **G**ain students' attention.
- **R**eview key details from the most recent lesson (if applicable).
- Clearly state the **O**bjective of the lesson:
  - □ "Today's lesson is about using basic note-taking guidelines to improve the quality of your notes regardless of the subject matter you're studying."
- Explain **W**hy students should learn the information.
  - □ Explain to students that note taking is a skill that is required in most, if not all, of their classes. The better they are at taking notes, the more useful their notes will be when it's time to prepare for assignments, quizzes and exams.
  - □ Stress to students that note taking is for their OWN use and benefit. They should write notes in a way that makes sense to them and will be understandable when they review their notes at a later date.

Teacher Input/Modeling

- Use direct instruction to explain note-taking guidelines.
  - □ Use the Note-Taking Guidelines overhead to explain basic note taking. Encourage students to take notes while you introduce each guideline. Ask students to give you examples of symbols, abbreviations, and note-taking formats before revealing the examples listed on the overhead.

Guided/Independent Practice

- Have students take out a sheet of paper and practice note taking during your lecture. Walk around the room and check their notes to see if they are following the guidelines you're explaining.

Closure/Review

- Ask for at least three volunteers to share their notes with the class. Discuss the note-taking guidelines that each of them followed. Point out any shorthand, symbols, or abbreviations they used. An example might be a student who wrote "info" in place of "information."

- Let students practice independently by giving them an article (choose any from those on pages 90-103) to read and take notes from.

Connection/Extension

- This lesson complements all of the lessons related to note-taking formats, as well as any classroom activities or assignments that require note taking.

Note-Taking Guidelines

- Several ways to take notes
- Notes are for YOU
- Make notes clear and useful to YOU
- Always include a heading on your notes
- Choose information that you think is important and put information in a useful order
- Don't use complete sentences
- Single words can take the place of phrases
- Write number words as numerals (one = 1)
- Use symbols to make notes shorter and note taking faster
  - #, %, @, $, &, =, +, -, ↑, ↓
- Use abbreviations to make notes brief
  - w/o, U.S.A., Oct., vocab.
- Know what the topic or subject is before deciding how to take notes
- Choose a note-taking format that works best for the topic and for YOU
  - bulleted list
  - T-charts
  - spider web
  - others:

Using Abbreviations

OBJECTIVE

Students will be able to use abbreviations to improve the speed and ease of their note taking while listening to a lecture.

MATERIALS

Overhead or LCD projector

Overhead
Using Abbreviations during
   Note Taking

Worksheet (one per student)
Using Abbreviations during
   Note Taking

Answer Key Overhead
Using Abbreviations during
   Note Taking

APPROXIMATE TIME

10 minutes

Introduction

- **G**ain students' attention.
- **R**eview key details from the most recent lesson (if applicable).
- Clearly state the **O**bjective of the lesson:
  - "The purpose of today's lesson is to learn how to use abbreviations so you can improve the speed and ease of your note taking."
- Explain **W**hy students should learn the information.
  - Explain to students that learning how to abbreviate words while taking notes allows them to write more quickly. Abbreviations are a form of shorthand that saves time, which makes keeping up with a teacher or speaker much easier.

Teacher Input/Modeling

- Use direct instruction to explain what abbreviations are and how to apply them.
  - Write the following phrase on the board or an overhead: Tk nts using abbr.
  - Call on students to decipher the phrase until someone reads it correctly. (If students can't provide the correct answer, tell the class it is an abbreviation of the phrase: Take notes using abbreviations.) Explain to the class that the best abbreviations are easy to figure out and make sense whenever you see them. Ask students to give examples of any common abbreviations they've used before. After a brief discussion, show the Using Abbreviations during Note Taking overhead to explain how to abbreviate.

Guided/Independent Practice

■ Distribute the worksheets and have students practice guided note taking by filling in the blanks as you present from the overhead.

    □ When you get to the examples, do the first example as a group, and then have students work independently to answer the remaining two examples. Instruct students to write abbreviations for the 10 words on the second page of their worksheet, based on the guidelines just discussed.

Closure/Review

■ Use the Using Abbreviations during Note Taking Answer Key overhead to review students' worksheets, either at the end of the lesson or the following day.

■ At the end of the lesson, have students turn to each other and describe two different ways to write abbreviations. Call on students to share their answers aloud.

Connection/Extension

■ You can extend this lesson by assigning students an article to read and have them take notes using abbreviations.

Using Abbreviations during Note Taking

Why use Abbreviations:

Saves time

No memorizing, if done right

How to Abbreviate:

Use the following methods to abbreviate words so you know what the abbreviation stands for the next time you see it.

- **Use the first few letters of the word.**
  October - Oct
  President - pres
  Vocabulary - vocab

- **Leave out the vowels.**
  Book - bk
  Students - stdnt
  School - schl

- **Use the first letter of each syllable.**
  Notebook - nb
  Worksheet - ws

Using Abbreviations during Note Taking

Name: _____ Date: _____

Why use Abbreviations:

_____

_____

_____

How to Abbreviate:

Use the following methods to abbreviate so that you know what the abbreviation means the next time you see it.

■ _____

EXAMPLES:

October -

President -

Vocabulary -

■ _____

EXAMPLES:

Book -

Students -

School -

■ _____

EXAMPLES:

Notebook -

Worksheet -

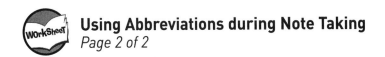

Using Abbreviations during Note Taking
Page 2 of 2

Below is a list of 10 commonly used words. After each word, write an abbreviation based on the guidelines just discussed. Choose the guideline that makes the most sense to you – after all, they're your notes!

1. homework _____

2. December _____

3. Missouri _____

4. biology _____

5. government _____

6. test _____

7. read _____

8. library _____

9. problem _____

10. chapter _____

Using Abbreviations during Note Taking

(answers may vary)

1.	homework	hw, hmwk
2.	December	Dec.
3.	Missouri	Mo
4.	biology	bio, blgy
5.	government	gov, gvmt
6.	test	tst
7.	read	rd
8.	library	lib, lbry
9.	problem	prob, pb
10.	chapter	chapt, chptr

Using Symbols

OBJECTIVE

Students will be able to identify common symbols and use them to simplify the note-taking process.

MATERIALS

Overhead or LCD projector

Overheads
What Does It Mean?
What Is the Symbol?

Worksheets (one per student)
What Does It Mean?
What Is the Symbol?

Answer Key Overheads
What Does It Mean?
What Is the Symbol?

APPROXIMATE TIME

10 minutes

Introduction

- **G**ain students' attention.
- **R**eview key details from the most recent lesson (if applicable).
- Clearly state the **O**bjective of the lesson:
  - □ "Symbols can have the same meaning as words and phrases. Today's lesson is about using symbols in note taking so you can save time and effort, which is helpful when you're trying to keep pace with a fast-talking teacher or speaker."
- Explain **W**hy students should learn the information.
  - □ Ask students, "Raise your hand if you've ever written an IM (instant message) or text message before?" (Most hands should go up.) Ask students if they type out their messages word-for-word, or if they use short-hand to express their thoughts. After a brief discussion, point out that many of them are already using symbols and abbreviations, and today's lesson is about how symbols can simplify the note-taking process.

Teacher Input/Modeling

- Use direct instruction to define what symbols are and provide examples of common symbols.
  - □ Start a brief discussion about symbols. Define symbols as marks or signs that represent something. Tell students that numbers, punctuation marks, mathematical/scientific signs, or even pictures can be symbols. Explain that 411 is a numeric symbol that means "information." Ask students what symbols they've used before or are familiar with. Write their answers on the board or an overhead. If students need help coming up with examples, prompt them to think about instant messages or text messages.

Guided/Independent Practice

- Divide students into two groups. In group one, give each student a copy of the "What Does It Mean?" worksheet. Instruct them to write down what each symbol stands for, using the space provided on their worksheet. Give each student in group two a copy of the "What Is the Symbol?" worksheet. Instruct them to write down the symbol that represents each word or phrase, using the space provided on their worksheet.

  - When everyone is finished, or has answered as many as they can, pair students from group one with students from group two. In pairs, have students compare answers and make corrections as needed. Ask for volunteers to share their answers, and use the answer key overheads to show the correct words and symbols.

Closure/Review

- Summarize the lesson with a review of three or four of the most difficult or challenging symbols. Have individual students draw the symbols on an overhead or the board.

Connection/Extension

- To extend the lesson, you can assign students an article to read and have them take notes using symbols. This lesson also complements the lesson on using abbreviations and can lead into a discussion about the gleaning strategy, which involves using symbols, abbreviations, and shorthand together. Information and guidelines on the gleaning strategy are available from this Web site: http://fates.cns.muskingum.edu/~cal/database/general/notetaking4.html

What Does It Mean?

Name: _____ Date: _____

SYMBOL	MEANING
411	
*	
#	
%	
@	
≈	
©	
≠	
<	
=	
>	
$	
↑	
↓	
¶	
e.g.	
&	
w/	
w/o	
?	
2	
**	
+	
-	

What Is the Symbol?

Name: _____ Date: _____

SYMBOL	MEANING
	information
	percent, percentage
	at
	up, increase
	down, decrease
	for example
	with
	without
	and
	about, approximately
	plus, in addition
	minus, not including
	two, too, to
	money, dollar
	greater than
	less than
	equal
	important
	very important
	copyright
	number
	not equal
	paragraph
	question

What Does It Mean?

SYMBOL	MEANING
411	information
*	important
#	number
%	percent, percentage
@	at
≈	about, approximately
©	copyright
≠	not equal
<	less than
=	equal
>	greater than
$	money, dollars
↑	up, increase
↓	down, decrease
¶	paragraph
e.g.	for example
&	and
w/	with
w/o	without
?	question
2	two, too, to
**	very important
+	plus, in addition
-	minus, not including

Lesson 4: Answer Key Overhead

What Is the Symbol?

SYMBOL	MEANING
411	information
%	percent, percentage
@	at
↑	up, increase
↓	down, decrease
e.g.	for example
w/	with
w/o	without
&	and
≈	about, approximately
+	plus, in addition
-	minus, not including
2	two, too, to
$	money, dollar
>	greater than
<	less than
=	equal
*	important
**	very important
©	copyright
#	number
≠	not equal
¶	paragraph
?	question

LESSON 5

Using the '5 W's and How' Note-Taking Method

OBJECTIVE

Students will be able to use the "5 W's and How" note-taking method to determine the main ideas of an article or printed text.

MATERIALS

Overhead or LCD projector

Worksheet (one per student)
"5 W's and How" Method

Articles (one per student)
American Revolution, pg. 90
Denim Jeans, pg. 93

Answer Key Overheads
American Revolution
Denim Jeans

APPROXIMATE TIME

10 minutes

Introduction

- **G**ain students' attention.
- **R**eview key details from the most recent lesson (if applicable).
- Clearly state the **O**bjective of the lesson:
  - □ "In today's lesson, you will practice using the '5 W's and How' note-taking method and learn why it can help you determine the main ideas of a story or reading assignment."
- Explain **W**hy students should learn the information.
  - □ Point out to students that the best notes are those that capture critical pieces of information, and the "5 W's and How" is one way they can zero in on content that is important to know and learn.
  - □ Describe how this strategy will focus their attention on key facts and main ideas so they're not wasting time or effort with irrelevant or unimportant content.

Teacher Input/Modeling

- Use direct instruction to introduce students to the "5 W's and How" method.
  - □ Ask students, "Raise your hand if you have heard of the American Revolution or the Revolutionary War?" (You should see most hands go up.) Follow up by asking, "If I were to test your knowledge about this war, what questions do you think I might ask?" (Responses should include: Who fought, when it took place, where it was fought, who won, how many casualties, etc. You may have to guide students toward these types of questions if they need help.) Point out that such questions relate to facts, and the "5 W's and How" note-taking method can help them identify important facts and information.

- Define what the "5 W's" stand for, and tell students that they are going to pick out the most important facts and details using this method.

Guided/Independent Practice

- Have students complete a "5 W's and How" worksheet while reading about the American Revolution.

  ☐ Give each student a copy of the "5 W's and How" Method worksheet and a copy of the *American Revolution* article. Instruct them to read the article and answer the who, what, when, where, why, and how questions. If students need guidance, you may read the first paragraph aloud and identify any main ideas. Be sure to review students' worksheets to check the accuracy of their notes.

Closure/Review

- Summarize the lesson by having students turn to a partner and say what the "5 W's" and the "H" stand for. Call on several students to answer aloud, then finish with a reminder that this note-taking method will help them identify the main ideas in their reading assignments.

- If you feel students need more guided or independent practice, have students read the *Denim Jeans* article and take notes using the "5 W's and How" method (distribute additional copies of the worksheet for student notes).

Connection/Extension

- You can connect this lesson to a lesson on writing summaries. After students take notes using the "5 W's and How" format, explain that they've successfully identified the main ideas of an article. Have them use their notes to write a summary of what they've read.

"5 W's and How" Method

Name: _____ Date: _____

TOPIC: _____

Who?	
What?	
When?	
Where?	
Why?	
How?	

'5 W's and How' Method

TOPIC: _____ American Revolution

Who?	America's 13 colonies and Great Britain
What?	Colonists rebelled over British laws and their victory resulted in independent U.S.A.
When?	April 19, 1775 to 1781
Where?	13 colonies Battles of Lexington & Concord in Mass. Started it Battle of Yorktown, Va. Ended it Treaty of Paris signed 1783 officially ended it
Why?	Colonists thought Stamp and Townshend Acts were unfair and repressive
How?	How did it turn out? Colonists won Representatives wrote the Declaration of Independence which was adopted July 4, 1776

'5 W's and How' Method

TOPIC: _____Denim Jeans_____

Who?	Levi Strauss, David Jacobs
What?	Copper rivets were added to work pants Pants made out of sturdy cotton called denim Many varieties today
When?	1873
Where?	San Francisco
Why?	Wanted more durable work pants
How?	Became popular & sold worldwide

Taking Notes Using the Cornell Method

OBJECTIVE

Students will be able to use the Cornell Method of note taking to select main ideas and supporting details from text.

MATERIALS

Overhead or LCD projector

Overhead
Cornell Method of Note Taking

Worksheet (one per student)
Cornell Method of Note Taking

Articles (one per student)
The Color Wheel, pg. 100
The Sport of Polo, pg. 102

Answer Key Overheads
The Color Wheel
The Sport of Polo

APPROXIMATE TIME

10 minutes

Introduction

- **G**ain students' attention.
- **R**eview key details from the most recent lesson (if applicable).
- Clearly state the **O**bjective of the lesson:
    - "In today's lesson, you will learn how to organize your notes using the Cornell Method. You'll also practice using this strategy by taking notes from an article."
- Explain **W**hy students should learn the information.
    - Ask students, "Raise your hand if you have ever reviewed your notes but couldn't find the information you needed because your notes were messy, or they were not organized in a logical way?" (Most students will raise their hands.) Explain that the Cornell Method will help them structure their notes in a consistent way. This can be especially useful when they're taking notes from a textbook and are confused or unsure about the content. Also mention that the Cornell Method makes it easier to review and understand old notes, taken days or weeks earlier.

Teacher Input/Modeling

- Use direct instruction to define the Cornell Method and how it is used.
- Use the Cornell Method of Note Taking overhead to highlight the method's format and steps. Have students follow along by filling in their Cornell Method worksheet (distributed earlier). Periodically ask questions to check for understanding. Ask students to complete the final step of the Cornell Method – writing a summary – at the bottom of their worksheets. Check for understanding by walking around and reviewing each student's summary.

Guided/Independent Practice

■ Have students take out a sheet of notebook paper, then give them a copy of either *The Color Wheel* or *The Sport of Polo* article (whichever you choose to use). Instruct students to read the article and take notes using the Cornell Method.

Closure/Review

■ Have students work in pairs to review each other's notes. Tell students to double check how many of the eight formatting steps were followed correctly.

■ If students need additional practice, assign another article and have students take notes using the Cornell Method.

Connection/Extension

■ To extend the lesson, you can do an exercise on basic outlining because the Cornell Method encourages the use of headings and numbers.

■ This lesson also complements the lesson plan on using abbreviations because the Cornell Method encourages students to shorten words.

Cornell Method of Note Taking

TOPIC: Cornell Method

Main Ideas	
What is it? (3)	A structured format for note taking
	An easy way to organize main ideas and supporting details
	Applies to both printed text and oral lectures
How to use it: (8)	Use notebook paper
	One side only
	Divide paper w/ line about 2 inches from left
	Write short headings on the left, such as "main ideas" and "key words"
	Write details on the right
	Leave space at bottom to summarize
	Fill in space on the left with the number of details
	Fold back the right side of the page to quiz yourself
Summary:	

Cornell Method of Note Taking

Name: _____ Date: _____

TOPIC: _____

Main Ideas

What is it?

How to use it:

Summary:

The Color Wheel

TOPIC: The Color Wheel

Color Wheel **(3)**	Circular diagram Divided into colors ☐ Used to see relationship between colors & color combos
Primary Colors **(2)**	Red, blue, yellow ☐ Used to create all other colors
Secondary Colors **(2)**	Purple, green, orange ☐ Made by mixing 2 primary colors in equal amounts
Tertiary Colors **(2)**	Red-violet, blue-violet, Blue-green, yellow-green, yellow-orange, red-orange ☐ made by mixing primary & secondary colors
Complementary Colors **(3)**	Located opposite each other on the color wheel ☐ don't share any common colors ☐ used to show contrast
Colors next to each other **(2)**	☐ have a color in common ☐ ex: red, red-orange, orange (all have red in common)
Summary	The color wheel is a giant circle that is divided into colors. The colors that are placed next to each other have a color in common while colors that are on opposite sides from each other don't. The wheel is divided into primary, secondary, and tertiary colors.

The Sport of Polo

TOPIC: Polo

Game Play (5)	☐ indoor or outdoor ☐ players on horseback ☐ 2 teams of 4 players ☐ score more goals than the other team ☐ players use wooden mallet to hit the polo ball
Time (3)	☐ chukkers: 7-minute time periods ☐ six chukkers in a match ☐ players change horses after each period
Starting (1)	☐ umpire rolls the ball on the field at each chukker & after each goal
Halftime (1)	☐ spectators "divot stomp"; they stomp down turf that horses have torn up
Field (1)	☐ 300 x 160 yd (nine football fields)
Summary:	Polo is a team sport played by hitting a ball with a wooden mallet while on horseback. The game has 6 time periods and at halftime spectators help stomp divots torn up by horses. At the end, the team with the most goals wins.

Using a T-Chart

OBJECTIVE

Students will be able to correctly identify a T-chart, recognize situations when a T-chart is the most appropriate note-taking format, and use a T-chart to take notes from printed text.

Materials
Overhead or LCD projector

Overheads
Positives and Negatives of
  Watching TV
Guidelines for Using a T-Chart

Worksheet (two per student)
T-Chart Notes

Articles (one per student)
Insects and Spiders, pg. 95
Babe Ruth, pg. 91
The Seven (or Six) Continents, pg. 101

Answer Key Overheads
Insects and Spiders
Babe Ruth
The Seven (or Six) Continents

APPROXIMATE TIME

20 minutes

Introduction

- **G**ain students' attention.
- **R**eview key details from the most recent lesson (if applicable).
- Clearly state the **O**bjective of the lesson:
  - "Today's lesson is all about the T-chart. We're going to define what it is, learn how and when to use it, and then practice taking notes using a T-chart format."
- Explain **W**hy students should learn the information.
  - Point out that notes written on T-charts are easy to follow and specific information can be found quickly and easily during study reviews.
  - Show the class the Positives and Negatives of Watching TV overhead. Ask students to tell you good things and not so good things about television viewing. (Answers should reflect what's written on the overhead.)
  - Follow up by asking the class why it was so easy for them to know the positives and negatives. (Answers should include how information was divided into two columns and headings were used.) Explain that the pros and cons were organized using a T-chart, and today they're going to practice taking notes using the same strategy.

Teacher Input/Modeling

- Use direct instruction to explain what, when, and how to use a T-chart.
  - Display the Guidelines for Using a T-Chart overhead to show what a T-chart looks like and when it's an appropriate format to use. Ask students to share their own experiences making or using a T-chart. Have students

follow along with the lecture by taking notes using one of their T-Chart Notes worksheets (distributed earlier).

Guided/Independent Practice

- Instruct students to read the *Insects and Spiders, Babe Ruth,* or *The Seven (or Six) Continents* article (whichever you choose to use) and take notes using a T-chart format. (Students can use their second T-Chart worksheet for note taking, or you can have them draw their own T-chart.)

- Before they begin, have students scan the article, then as a class, discuss why a T-chart is an appropriate strategy for this reading assignment. If you feel students need more guidance, help them identify and label main headings for their T-chart.

Closure/Review

- Use the appropriate answer key overhead to review students' T-chart notes, either at the end of the lesson or the following day.

- Summarize the lesson by having students work with a partner to identify at least three situations that are appropriate for using a T-chart. Call on groups to share their answers.

- If students need additional practice, assign another article and have students take notes using a T-chart format.

Connection/Extension

- To extend the lesson, have students compare and contrast two objects. Explain how a T-chart is a convenient way to group facts and details that are related, and then have students write a compare and contrast essay based on their T-chart notes.

Topic: The Positives and Negatives of Watching TV

POSITIVES	NEGATIVES
■ Keep up on world events	■ Inappropriate programs
■ Weather updates	■ Violence
■ News	■ Adult content
■ Educational programs	■ Creates "couch potatoes"
■ Provides entertainment	■ Takes away quality time from family
■ Relaxing	

Guidelines for Using a T-Chart

TYPES OF NOTES: T-Chart

Useful for:

- ☐ Cause and Effect
- ☐ Compare and Contrast
- ☐ Important Dates and What Happened
- ☐ Words and Definitions
- ☐ Advantages and Disadvantages

Why use a T-chart:

- ☐ Notes are organized
- ☐ Notes are brief (no space for complete sentences)
- ☐ Notes are in your own words
- ☐ Notes are side by side, making them easy to compare
- ☐ Format allows you to create an easy study guide (cover up one column and use the other column as clue words)
- ☐ Captures the most important details (irrelevant details are left out because of limited space)

T-Chart Notes

Name: _____ Date: _____

TOPIC: _____

Insects and Spiders

TOPIC: _____ **Insects and Spiders** _____

INSECTS	SPIDERS
■ Outer skeleton	■ Outer skeleton
■ Body: ☐ Head ☐ Thorax ☐ Abdomen (end)	■ Body ☐ Head ☐ Abdomen
■ 6 legs	■ 8 legs
■ 2 antennae	■ No antennae
■ Winged: ☐ Butterflies, mosquitoes	■ No wings
■ Wingless: ☐ Fleas	■ Venomous w/ fangs
■ All habitats	■ Eat insects ☐ Scorpion, tarantula, ticks ☐ Arachnids
■ Up to 2.5 oz	■ All habitats
	■ Up to 3.0 oz

Answers or notes will vary, but they should be brief. Students should not write complete sentences; abbreviations and symbols should be used when applicable.

Babe Ruth

TOPIC: _____ **Babe Ruth** _____

DATE/AGE	EVENT
2/6/1895	Born Baltimore, MD
Age 7	Reform school/ Boys orphanage
Age 19	Signed w/ Boston Red Sox Got nickname "Babe" Moved to majors 6 yrs pitching
1919	Went to NY Yankees Record 54 home runs 1st yr
lifetime	Home run leader 12 times 3 home runs in 2 World Series games Career home runs: 714

Answers or notes will vary, but they should be brief. Students should not write complete sentences; abbreviations and symbols should be used when applicable.

The Seven (or Six) Continents

TOPIC: __The Seven Continents__

CONTINENTS	DESCRIPTION
Africa	Size: 2nd largest Population: 840 million, Over 50 nations Outstanding features: Nile River, natural resources, wildlife Other: famine, disease, poverty, civil wars
Antarctica	Population: < 200,000 have been there Features: cold, dry, mostly ice Other: Scientists study climate change
Asia	Size: largest, 17 million mi² Population: 3 out of 5 people live there
Australia/Oceania	Size: Smallest Population: 20 million Other: Most live on the coast
Europe	Population: 800 million, over 40 nations Features: separated from Asia by Ural Mts.
N. America	Population: Over 20 nations Area: Panama to Greenland
S. America	Features: The Amazon Rainforest, Isthmus of Panama

Answers or notes will vary, but they should be brief. Students should not write complete sentences; abbreviations and symbols should be used when applicable.

Creating Concept Maps

OBJECTIVE

Students will be able to create and use concept maps to write more visual and readable notes taken from printed text.

MATERIALS

Overhead or LCD projector

Overheads
Guided Practice – Spider Web
Guided Practice – Compare and
    Contrast
Guided Practice – Flowchart
Guidelines for Constructing
    Spider Webs

Worksheet (one per student)
Guided Practice – Spider Web

Articles (one per student)
Lie Detector, pg. 96
Oprah Winfrey, pg. 97

Answer Key Overheads
Lie Detector
Oprah Winfrey

APPROXIMATE TIME

15 minutes

Introduction

- **G**ain students' attention.
- **R**eview key details from the most recent lesson (if applicable).
- Clearly state the **O**bjective of the lesson:
  - ☐ "Today, you're going to learn about concept maps. You will see three different variations of concept maps and practice taking notes using one called a spider web."
- Explain **W**hy students should learn the information.
  - ☐ Explain to students that most people can recall images faster and easier than the words they read on a page. Many even remember pictures longer than they remember written words. That's why knowing how to convert notes into concept maps can be so beneficial. A concept map can trick your brain into thinking your notes are actually an image, making the information easier to recall.
  - ☐ Ask students if they are familiar with the phrase, "A picture is worth a thousand words"? Start a discussion about the meaning of that proverb (comment on how a powerful image can express an idea or emotion more clearly than words often can and how visualization can help them absorb information quickly). End the class discussion by telling students that they are going to learn how to make their notes more visual and memorable by using concept maps.

Teacher Input/Modeling

- Use direct instruction to explain and define concept maps. Use the guided practice overheads to show a visual depiction of the spider web, compare and contrast, and flowchart concept maps. (The remaining instructions in this lesson focus on spider webs.)

ADDITIONAL MATERIALS FOR FLOWCHART AND COMPARE AND CONTRAST CONCEPT MAPS

Overheads
Guidelines for Constructing Compare and Contrast Concept Maps
Guidelines for Constructing Flowcharts

Worksheets (one per student)
Guided Practice – Compare and Contrast
Guided Practice – Flowchart

Articles (one per student)
Insects and Spiders, pg. 95
Digesting Food, pg. 94
Papermaking Process, pg. 98

Answer Key Overheads
Insects and Spiders Compare and Contrast Concept Map
Digesting Food Flowchart
Papermaking Process Flowchart

■ Define concept maps as visual illustrations that connect supporting details with main ideas. Explain to students that the term "spider web" refers to a note-taking design in which the main idea is written in the center of a note page or diagram – just like a spider sitting in its web – and the supporting details are written around the main idea. Use the Guidelines for Constructing Spider Webs overhead to explain how a spider web is made.

Guided/Independent Practice

■ After reviewing the guidelines, build a spider web with your class.

  □ Work from the Guided Practice overhead, and have students follow along using their Guided Practice worksheet (distributed earlier). Begin by writing the words "Styles of Music" in the center box on the overhead (students should do the same on their worksheets). Ask students to name different styles of music, then write their responses (if accurate) next to the lines extending out from the center box (students should do the same). Call on students to give examples of each musical style listed (singer, song, etc.). Write their examples near the style of music it relates to, then draw a line connecting the example with the style.

■ Congratulate the students for successfully making a spider web, then say they are now ready to make one on their own.

  □ Instruct students to read the *Lie Detector* or *Oprah Winfrey* article (whichever you choose to use) and take notes using a spider web format.

Closure/Review

■ Use the appropriate answer key overhead to review students' spider web notes, either at the end of the lesson or the following day. Discuss the article's main ideas and supporting details.

■ At the end of the lesson, verbally quiz the students by asking them to recall the guidelines for making a spider web concept map.

Connection/Extension

- You can extend this lesson by doing a second spider web exercise or introducing another design format (flowchart or compare and contrast) using guided practice. The necessary support materials are provided at the end of this lesson.

Guided Practice – Spider Web

Name: _____ Date: _____

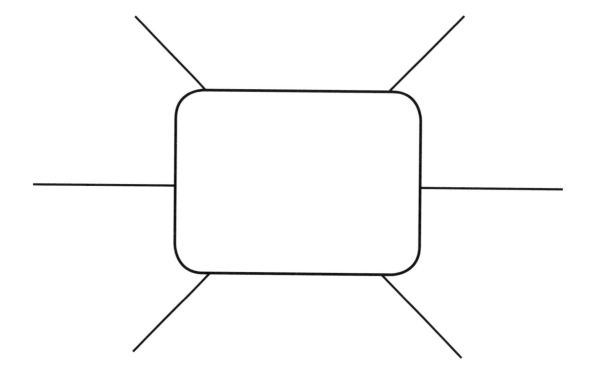

Guidelines for Constructing Spider Webs

- Identify the main idea and write it down in the middle of the page.

- Draw a circle or square around the main idea.

- Identify subtopics.

- Draw a line out from the main idea and write the subtopic next to the line, then draw a circle or square around the subtopic.

- Repeat the previous step until all subtopics are written down and circled.

- Identify any supporting details, and draw lines connecting them to the appropriate subtopic.

- Keep notes short and brief (no complete sentences on a spider web).

Lie Detector

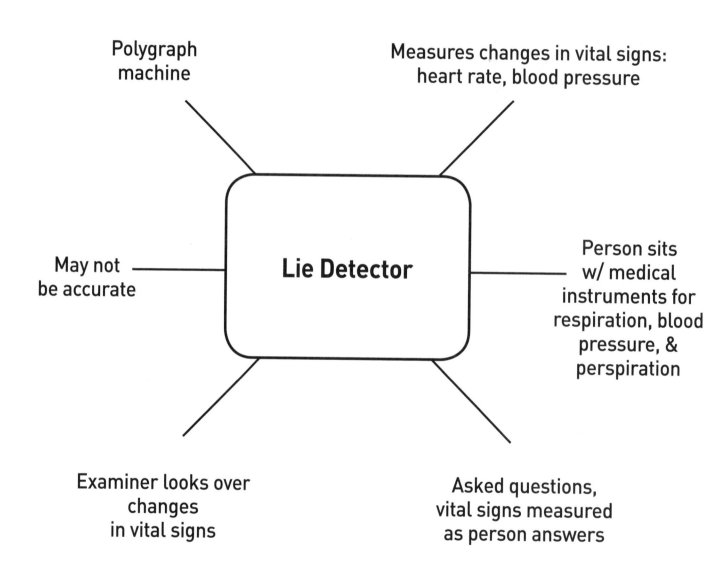

Polygraph machine

Measures changes in vital signs: heart rate, blood pressure

May not be accurate

Lie Detector

Person sits w/ medical instruments for respiration, blood pressure, & perspiration

Examiner looks over changes in vital signs

Asked questions, vital signs measured as person answers

Oprah Winfrey

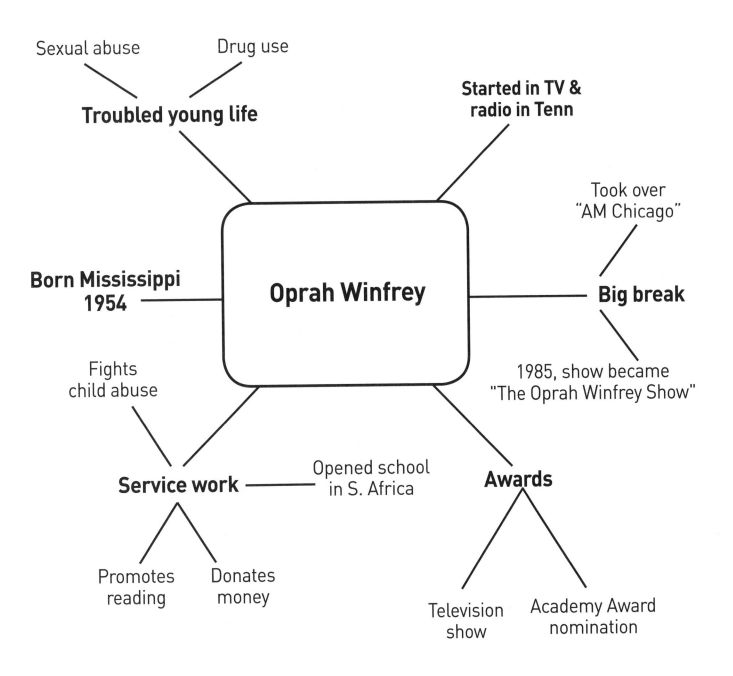

Sexual abuse   Drug use

Troubled young life

Started in TV & radio in Tenn

Took over "AM Chicago"

Born Mississippi 1954

Oprah Winfrey

Big break

1985, show became "The Oprah Winfrey Show"

Fights child abuse

Service work —— Opened school in S. Africa

Awards

Promotes reading   Donates money

Television show   Academy Award nomination

Compare and Contrast Concept Maps

- Identify the two topics that will be compared and contrasted.

- Construct a T-chart.

- Write one topic as the heading on the left side of the chart.

- Write the second topic as the heading on the right side of the chart.

- Use abbreviated notes to write key details about each topic.

- Draw a box at the bottom of the T-chart. (Use about one-quarter of the page.)

- Label the left side of the box "similarities" and the right side of the box "differences."

- Review your notes to find similarities between the two topics and then record them on the left side of the box.

- Review your notes to find differences between the two topics and then record them on the right side of the box.

Guided Practice – Compare and Contrast

Name: _____ Date: _____

TOPIC ONE	TOPIC TWO

SIMILARITIES	DIFFERENCES
1.	1.
2.	2.
3.	3.
4.	4.

Lesson 8: Worksheet

©2008, Father Flanagan's Boys' Home

69

COMPARE AND CONTRAST CONCEPT MAP
Insects and Spiders

INSECTS	SPIDERS
■ Outer skeleton	■ Outer skeleton
■ Body:	■ Body
□ Head	□ Head
□ Thorax	□ Abdomen
□ Abdomen (end)	■ 8 legs
■ 6 legs	■ No antennae
■ 2 antennae	■ No wings
■ Winged:	■ Venomous w/ fangs
□ Butterflies, mosquitoes	□ Eat insects
■ Wingless:	□ Scorpion, tarantula, ticks
□ Fleas	■ Arachnids
■ All habitats	■ All habitats
■ Up to 2.5 oz	■ Up to 3.0 oz

SIMILARITIES
1. Outer skeleton
2. Wingless varieties
3. All habitats

DIFFERENCES
1. spiders only have head & thorax
2. different # of legs
3. spiders have no antennae

Lesson 8: Answer Key Overhead

Guidelines for Constructing Flowcharts

- Flowcharts are best for organizing material that has several steps or stages.

- Identify the main idea, and then write it down at the top of the page.

- Draw a circle or square around the main idea.

- Identify the first step, and then write it down under the main idea.

- Draw a circle or square around the first step.

- Use an arrow to connect the main idea and the first step.

- Continue to identify the most important steps in the process, and write them down in the order they occur.

- Be sure to connect all the steps using arrows that indicate the relationship, such as what happens first or what is a result.

- You may label the arrows with descriptive words to provide clarification.

- Write a brief summary of the process below your flow chart when you are finished.

- Keep steps short and brief (use abbreviations and symbols; do not use complete sentences).

Guided Practice – Flowchart

Name: _____ Date: _____

SUMMARY:

Digesting Food Flowchart

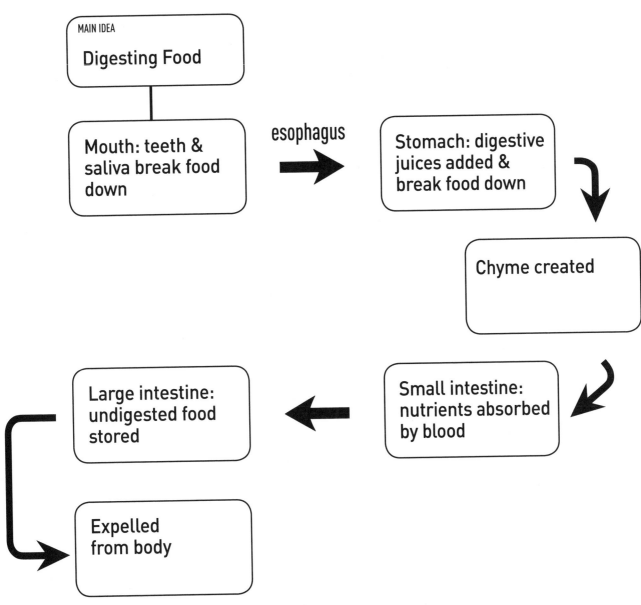

MAIN IDEA

Digesting Food

Mouth: teeth & saliva break food down

esophagus

Stomach: digestive juices added & break food down

Chyme created

Large intestine: undigested food stored

Small intestine: nutrients absorbed by blood

Expelled from body

SUMMARY: Digestion starts in the mouth where the teeth and saliva begin to break food down. Next, the food goes down the esophagus to the stomach where it is broken down further by digestive juices and becomes a substance called chyme. Next, it's on to the small intestine where nutrients are absorbed and anything that cannot be absorbed goes to the large intestine to be expelled.

Papermaking Process Flowchart

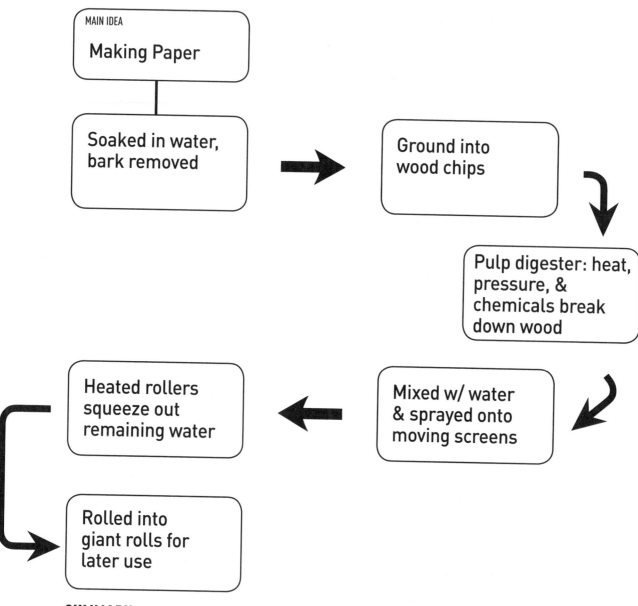

MAIN IDEA
Making Paper

Soaked in water, bark removed

Ground into wood chips

Pulp digester: heat, pressure, & chemicals break down wood

Mixed w/ water & sprayed onto moving screens

Heated rollers squeeze out remaining water

Rolled into giant rolls for later use

SUMMARY: To make paper, logs are soaked in water to remove the bark. Next, wood chips are made and placed into a pulp digester where heat, pressure, and chemicals break the wood down further to create pulp that must be cleaned. Water is mixed in and the new mixture is sprayed onto screens where heated rollers squeeze out water and press the pulp into sheets. The sheets are rolled into giant rolls to be used later.

Lesson 8: Answer Key Overhead

Using a Four-Square

Students will be able to use the four-square note-taking method, recognize situations when a four-square is the most appropriate format, and use a four-square to take notes from printed text.

MATERIALS

Overhead or LCD projector

Overhead
What Is a Four-Square?

Worksheet (one per student)
Four-Square

Articles (one per student)
Venomous Snakes, pg. 103
Styles of Music, pg. 99

Answer Key Overheads
Venomous Snakes
Styles of Music

APPROXIMATE TIME

10 minutes

Introduction

- **G**ain students' attention.
- **R**eview key details from the most recent lesson (if applicable).
- Clearly state the **O**bjective of the lesson:
  - ☐ "Today, we're going to define the four-square note-taking method, learn how and when to use it, and then practice taking notes using a four-square."
- Explain **W**hy students should learn the information.
  - ☐ Explain to students that when they write their notes in a four-square format, information is easier to find because related facts and key details are grouped together.
  - ☐ Point out that a four-square organizes notes in a very structured way, which is helpful when working on assignments or studying for exams. Instead of flipping through pages and pages of notes, all of the information they're looking for is arranged on a single page.

Teacher Input/Modeling

- Use direct instruction to explain the four-square method, including how and when to use it.
  - ☐ Instruct students to follow along and take notes as you explain the four-square format using the What is a Four-Square? overhead. Engage students by periodically asking questions.

Guided/Independent Practice

- Start a classroom discussion about how and when to use a four-square, then have students practice independently.
  - ☐ Instruct students to read the *Venomous Snakes* or *Styles of Music* article (whichever you choose to use) and take notes on their Four-Square worksheet.

Closure/Review

- Use the appropriate answer key overhead to review students' four-square notes, either at the end of the lesson or the following day.

- To summarize the lesson, explain how nicely the four-square format works when a subject or text has four main topics. Ask students to think of other situations in which a four-square is useful, then solicit responses. If they need help, tell them to think back to your earlier presentation and class discussion.

Connection/Extension

- You can extend the lesson by assigning another article to read and having students take notes using a four-square that they create.

- You also can connect the lesson to other academic tasks. For example, you can explain how to use a four-square as a planning sheet for writing assignments. You also can teach students how a four-square can logically divide the similarities and differences between two objects, making it easier to write compare and contrast essays.

What Is a Four-Square?

What?

■ A note-taking method that allows you to organize information into four distinct, easy-to-read sections.

Why?

■ Allows you to find specific information quickly and easily without having to flip through several pages of notes because the information is contained on one page.

How?

■ Divide a sheet of paper into four squares or sections (either by folding the paper in half, then in half again, or drawing a vertical line down the middle of the paper and a horizontal line across the middle of the paper).

■ Write each main idea as a heading in separate squares.

■ Write brief notes in a bulleted or numbered format under each heading. (Use symbols, abbreviations, incomplete sentences, etc.)

■ Modify the page to create more or fewer squares depending on the number of main ideas.

What Is a Four-Square? (continued)

When?

- If the text has more than one section, use one square for each section.

- If the lecture is multiple days, summarize each day's notes in one square.

- If the text has four different topics, use one square for each topic.

- If you want a planning sheet to write a five-paragraph essay: Use one square for the introduction, three squares for the body, and a fifth square for the conclusion, if needed.

- If you want to compare and contrast information: Put notes about topic A in one square. Write notes about topic B in a second square. Any similarities between topics A and B, put in a third square. Any differences between topics A and B, write in a fourth square.

- Other:

Four-Square

Name: _____ Date: _____

TOPIC: _____

Venomous Snakes

TOPIC: _____Venomous Snakes_____

Rattlesnakes

Home: N & S America, most in SW U.S. like Arizona

Other Facts: can swim, called pit vipers

Features: have heat sensors, beads at tip of tail that rattle

Coral Snakes

Home: 65 species worldwide, 2 species in U.S.

Features: black, red, & yellow stripes

Other facts: live underground, hide under rocks, logs, leaves

Copperhead Snakes

Home: E. and Central U.S.

Features: copper head, reddish-brown body, heat sensors on head

Other facts: ave. lifespan - 18 yrs

Cottonmouth Snakes

Home: streams, ponds, lakes, swamplands

Features: wide mouth w/ white lining

Other facts: called water moccasins, bare fangs, 30-48 in. long

Styles of Music

TOPIC: _____ Styles of Music _____

Jazz

Started in New Orleans, early 1900s

Combines African, European bands, & Gospel

Improvised style

Unexpected beats

Artists: Billie Holiday, Duke Ellington

Rock and Roll

Started in U.S., 1950s

Combines jazz, R&B, gospel, & country

Types: punk, heavy metal, grunge, pop

Artists: Chuck Berry, Elvis Presley

Country

Started in southern U.S.

Came from folk & hillbilly music

Honest, emotional lyrics

Musical sounds: fiddle, banjo, guitar, & harmonica

Artists: Johnny Cash, Patsy Cline

Classical

Started in Europe, 18th & 19th centuries

Performed in concert halls, orchestras, & operas

Composers: Beethoven, Mozart

Using a Vocabulary Tri-Fold

LESSON 10

OBJECTIVE

Students will be able to use the vocabulary tri-fold note-taking format to learn word definitions and take notes from printed text using a tri-fold.

MATERIALS

Overhead or LCD projector

Overheads
Vocabulary Tri-Fold Instructions
Vocabulary Tri-Fold Sample

Worksheet (one per student)
Vocabulary Tri-Fold

Article (one per student)
The Color Wheel, pg. 100

Answer Key Overhead
Vocabulary Tri-Fold Notes

APPROXIMATE TIME

10 minutes

Introduction

■ **G**ain students' attention.

■ **R**eview key details from the most recent lesson (if applicable).

■ Clearly state the **O**bjective of the lesson:

  □ "Today's lesson introduces a note-taking format known as the vocabulary tri-fold. The tri-fold method is ideal for learning technical terms or unfamiliar words that you find in printed text or hear during a lecture. We're going to discuss how and when to use a tri-fold, and then practice taking notes using this format."

■ Explain **W**hy students should learn the information.

  □ Reinforce the idea that the tri-fold method allows students to organize vocabulary terms and definitions in a format that makes studying, whether with a partner or alone, much easier to do.

Teacher Input/Modeling

■ Use direct instruction to explain and demonstrate how to use the tri-fold note-taking method.

  □ Instruct students to follow along and take notes as you teach the tri-fold method using the Vocabulary Tri-Fold Instructions overhead. Show students a visual depiction of the tri-fold format using the Vocabulary Tri-Fold Sample overhead.

Guided/Independent Practice

■ Instruct students to read *The Color Wheel* article and take notes on their Vocabulary Tri-Fold worksheet.

Closure/Review

- Use the Vocabulary Tri-Fold Notes Answer Key overhead to review students' notes from *The Color Wheel* article, either at the end of the lesson or the following day.

- To summarize the lesson, divide students into small groups and ask them to discuss the benefits of using a tri-fold. Call on groups to share their answers. Responses should include how the method makes reading technical terms easier to understand and study.

Connection/Extension

- To extend the lesson, start a discussion or do an exercise on how to prepare for exams. Point out how students can quiz themselves or each other using a vocabulary tri-fold. You also can discuss how a tri-fold is useful for highlighting other types of information, not just vocabulary terms.

Vocabulary Tri-Fold Instructions

The tri-fold method:

- Use a spiral notebook for all vocabulary terms, or keep sheets of loose-leaf paper in a separate notebook or folder.

- Fold or draw a line down a sheet of paper about one-third from the left margin.

- Record vocabulary words on the left side of the fold or line.

- Write the definition, example, or explanation to the right of the line or fold.

- Fold over the right side of the paper (about one-third from the right margin) so the definitions, examples, or explanations are hidden.

- The folded edge hides the definitions and allows you to quiz yourself over the vocabulary terms.

Vocabulary Tri-Fold Sample

Name: _____

Subject: _____

Chapter: _____

1. Word

Definition, example, explanation, etc.

2. Word

Definition, example, explanation, etc.

3. Word

Definition, example, explanation, etc.

F
O
L
D

Vocabulary Tri-Fold

Name: _____ Date: _____

Subject: _____

Chapter: _____

Word	Definition, example, explanation, etc.

Vocabulary Tri-Fold Notes

Word	Definition, example, explanation, etc.
1. Color Wheel	Circular diagram Divided into colors ☐ Used to see relationship between colors & color combos
2. Primary Colors	Red, blue, yellow ☐ Used to create all other colors
3. Secondary Colors	Purple, green, orange ☐ Made by mixing 2 primary colors in equal amounts
4. Tertiary Colors	Red-violet, blue-violet, Blue-green, yellow-green, Yellow-orange, red-orange ☐ Made by mixing primary & secondary colors
5. Complementary Colors	Located opposite each other on the color wheel ☐ Don't share any common colors ☐ Used to show contrast

Lesson 10: Answer Key Overhead

Section 1

ArTicLEs

Articles

American Revolution

The American Revolution, also called the American War of Independence, lasted from 1775 to 1783. The war was fought between America's original 13 colonies and Great Britain, and the colonists' victory created an independent United States of America.

The colonists rebelled against British rule after a series of laws had been passed that the colonists considered unfair and repressive. The Stamp Act, for example, required that colonists pay taxes on every piece of paper they used. The Townshend Acts imposed taxes on imported items, such as glass and tea. The colonists had little say in the passage of these and other laws, which created tension and unrest. Colonists adopted the slogan "no taxation without representation" to communicate their disapproval. The anger and frustration of the colonists erupted on April 19, 1775, with the Battles of Lexington and Concord in Massachusetts. These were the first of many skirmishes between British soldiers and colonists.

During the war, colonial leaders representing each of the colonies – Connecticut, Delaware, Georgia, Maryland, Massachusetts, New Hampshire, New Jersey, New York, North Carolina, Pennsylvania, Rhode Island, South Carolina, and Virginia – met and organized in a legislative body called the Continental Congress. Members of the Congress, including Thomas Jefferson and Benjamin Franklin, drafted the Declaration of Independence. The declaration was voted on and approved on July 2 and formally adopted on July 4, 1776.

The war, however, continued for several more years. The last decisive battle was fought at Yorktown, Virginia, in 1781. When British General Charles Cornwallis surrendered there to American and French troops, the war essentially ended. Officially, the American Revolution came to an end when the Treaty of Paris was signed in 1783. The treaty formally recognized the United States as an independent nation.

Today, the Fourth of July is a national holiday and celebrated in communities across the country with parades, festivals, and fireworks.

Babe Ruth

On February 6, 1895, George Herman Ruth, Jr. was born in Baltimore, Maryland. The son of saloon owners, he would become one of the most famous sports figures of all time.

Ruth's path to fame was not an easy one. He spent his earliest years on the street and in trouble. By age 7, his parents had had enough of his antics and sent him to a reform school and orphanage for boys. It was his home for the next 12 years, and the place where he perfected his baseball skills.

When Ruth was 19, he signed a contract to play for the Boston Red Sox's minor league baseball team. His teammates nicknamed him Babe, and he was forever known as Babe Ruth. After playing just five months in the minor leagues, he moved up to the Majors. For six years he pitched and played outfield for the Red Sox. Ruth was an imposing figure on the ball diamond, standing 6-foot-2 and weighing more than 200 pounds.

In December 1919, the Red Sox traded Ruth to the New York Yankees. His first season as a Yankee was remarkable. He set a new record for home runs in a season – 54. The old record of 29 also belonged to Ruth. His power at the plate created so much buzz, ticket sales and fan interest soared. The resulting success led the team to build Yankee Stadium, which is affectionately known as "The House that Ruth Built."

Ruth's baseball achievements include leading the American League in home runs 12 times, being the only player ever to hit three home runs in two different World Series games, and holding the record (which stood 39 years) for most career home runs (714).

His success on the diamond and his larger-than-life persona earned him several nicknames, including the Sultan of Swat, the Home Run King, and the Great Bambino. But for many baseball fans, he is simply and fondly remembered as The Babe.

福 和 貴 愛

Chinese Characters

Unlike the English language, which uses the letters of the alphabet to form words and communicate ideas, the Chinese language uses symbols or characters. Each character, standing alone or combined with others, represents an idea or thing. Some Chinese dictionaries contain more than 50,000 characters. However, many of those are rarely if ever used today. To read a current Chinese-language newspaper or magazine, it's estimated that a person needs to be familiar with or understand about 3,000 characters.

Most characters are written using eight basic strokes, such as left- and right-falling strokes, rising strokes, and hooks. Also, characters are drawn or written starting from top to bottom and left to right. The most basic characters can be written in one stroke but complex characters may require as many as 64. Regardless of how many strokes are needed to write or draw a character, each character should be uniform in size. In other words, all characters should use up the same amount of space on a paper no matter how many elements or strokes are needed to write the character.

The Chinese writing system is believed to be the oldest in the world. In 2007, archeologists discovered rock carvings dating back more than 8,000 years. These ancient symbols depicted images like the sun and moon. The depictions are very similar to the earliest forms of Chinese characters. Before this discovery, the oldest characters ever found were on 4,500-year-old pottery.

Denim Jeans

From the dusty ranches of West Texas to the bustling streets of Tokyo, no place is out of place for blue jeans. Durable, yet fashionable, they are a symbol of casual American style and culture.

Blue jeans come in low-rise, high-rise, skinny, relaxed, boot-cut, straight, speckled, torn, and with zippers or without. They can cost as little as 20 dollars or much more than 2,000. Such sophisticated styles and high-end prices represent a drastic change from the basic blue jean that was first introduced in the 1800s.

Levi Strauss and David Jacobs are credited by many as the original creators of blue jeans. In 1873 they patented "Improvement in Fastening Pocket-Openings," a design innovation that involved putting copper rivets on work pants to improve their durability. These new "waist overalls" (now called jeans) were made of denim, a soft but sturdy cotton fabric. San Francisco-based Levi Strauss & Company manufactured the overalls, which quickly became the top-selling pant in the western United States. It wasn't until the 1950s that the company began distributing its jeans nationwide.

The popularity of blue jeans grew substantially when young people saw their favorite actors, including James Dean and Marlon Brando, sporting them in movies and on television. People started to associate jeans with youthful rebellion and rugged individuality. Today, virtually everyone has at least one pair of jeans in their wardrobe, and they've become acceptable attire in many workplaces and at some formal events, even weddings.

Digesting Food

Food is fuel for the body. It contains vitamins and nutrients that energize the body and keep it fit and functioning. But before food can become fuel, it first must be broken down and digested.

The digestive process starts in the mouth. When you take a bite of food, your teeth tear it apart and break it down into smaller pieces. Saliva also helps moisten the food, making it easier to swallow. The saliva contains digestive enzymes that help break down the chemical components of food, like sugars and starches, into smaller molecules. When you swallow, food moves into the esophagus. The esophagus connects the throat to the stomach. At the end of the esophagus, there is a muscular valve that allows food to pass into the stomach. After food passes through, the valve tightens so no food or stomach acid can come back up into the esophagus.

The stomach contains digestive juices that continue the process of breaking down food. This process turns food into a thick liquid called chyme. Chyme passes from the stomach into the small intestine, where the digestive process continues and nutrients are absorbed and carried throughout the body by blood. Any indigestible material in the small intestine then moves into the large intestine, which is the final stage of digestion. This is where undigested matter is stored until it is expelled as waste from the body.

Insects and Spiders

Many people assume that spiders are a kind of insect. They are not. While insects and spiders have some similarities, for example, both wear their skeletons on the outside of their bodies, they have a number of differences that make them distinct creatures.

An insect's body has three sections or parts. There is a head, middle section (called the thorax), and an end section (called the abdomen). A spider's body only has two parts. There is the head/thorax and the abdomen. Insects have six legs and two antennae. Spiders have eight legs and no antennae. Most insects have wings; no spiders have wings. Also, spiders are venomous, have fangs, and prey on insects.

There are two main types of insects – wingless and winged. Butterflies and mosquitoes are examples of winged insects. Wingless insects include fleas and bristletails. Spiders belong to the animal family known as arachnids. Scorpions, ticks, and tarantulas are different kinds of spiders. The tarantula is the biggest spider in the world. The largest insects weigh around 2.5 ounces, and the largest spiders can weigh as much as 3 ounces. Insects and spiders live in nearly every type of habitat on the planet, including snow and hot sand.

Lie Detector

Contrary to popular belief, a polygraph machine (commonly referred to as a lie detector) cannot actually tell if a person is lying or telling the truth. Rather, the machine measures changes in a person's vital signs – heart rate, blood pressure, respiration, and perspiration – that may suggest he or she is trying to hide the truth or be deceptive. Deceptive behavior is associated with certain physiological responses, and those responses are what a polygraph machine measures.

During a polygraph exam, an individual sits in a chair with a blood pressure cuff around his or her upper arm, two rubber tubes strapped around the chest and abdomen, and fingerplates (called galvanometers) attached to two fingers. The fingerplates measure perspiration, and the rubber tubes measure breathing. Once all of the devices are connected, the individual is asked a series of questions by an examiner, who is sometimes referred to as a forensic psychophysiologist or FP. Many of the questions relate to the specific situation or issue being investigated. Other questions are more general and designed to test how a person reacts and processes information. When the question-and-answer period ends, the examiner evaluates the results to check for changes in the individual's physiological responses. If there are significant changes, it suggests possible deception.

Critics of lie detectors argue that changes in breathing, blood pressure, and perspiration may be the result of other emotions, including the stress of the exam itself, and not an indication of dishonesty. They also point out that the examiner may interpret the results incorrectly.

Because there is debate about the accuracy of polygraphs, one should not automatically assume that failing a lie detector test proves guilt or deception or that passing the test proves innocence or truth.

Oprah Winfrey

Oprah Winfrey is one of the most famous women in the world. She is a billionaire, hosts one of the most popular talk shows on television, and owns a huge media company. She has used her fame and fortune to help countless people. Most recently, she built a new school for poor girls in South Africa.

Winfrey was born in 1954 in Kosciusko, Mississippi. As a child, she lived with her mother and was sexually abused by male relatives. Later, she moved in with her father in Nashville, Tennessee. Her father was strict, and tried to keep his daughter on a good path. But Winfrey still struggled with drugs and rebellious behavior as a teen.

Winfrey began to change her ways once she entered Tennessee State University in 1971. She began working in radio and television in the Nashville area, then moved to Baltimore, Maryland, to host a TV talk show. Her big break came when she took over as host for *A.M. Chicago,* a faltering Chicago television talk show. Within months, the program was number one in the ratings and Winfrey shot to national fame. A year later, in 1985, the program was called *The Oprah Winfrey Show.*

That same year, she co-starred in the movie *The Color Purple.* Her performance earned her an Academy Award nomination. In 1986, *The Oprah Winfrey Show* became a national program with an audience of 10 million people. Winfrey then formed her own company, Harpo Productions, and bought the program. She became the first woman in broadcast history to own and produce her own talk show.

Winfrey has won many awards for her television career and her efforts to fight child abuse and help children and families in poverty. *Time* magazine has named her one of the 100 Most Influential People of the 20th Century. She also has been active in promoting books and reading.

In 2007, Winfrey opened the Oprah Winfrey Leadership Academy for Girls near Johannesburg, South Africa. The school took five years to build and cost $40 million.

Papermaking Process

It is estimated that each person in the United States uses more than 600 pounds of paper every year. That may not be so surprising when you consider that every time you read a book, wipe your nose using a tissue, or gift wrap a birthday present, paper is part of the experience.

While paper has many uses today, its original purpose was to make communication easier. Paper provided a smoother and more convenient way to write down thoughts and ideas, as opposed to using stone tablets or cave walls. Invented in China around 105 AD, the earliest form of paper was made from a mixture of mulberry tree bark, bamboo fiber, and water. Today, the materials needed to make paper are quite similar, but the production process is more efficient and technologically advanced.

Papermaking most often begins with tree logs, however other materials (cotton, linen rags, and wheat straw) are sometimes used. Turning logs into paper is a multi-step process. First, the logs are soaked in water and then the bark is removed. When the logs are debarked, they are chopped or ground into small wood chips. The wood chips are then put into a pulp digester. Many pulp digesters use heat, pressure, and chemicals to break down the wood. The digester helps separate the wood's cellulose fibers, which are needed to create paper, from other components in the wood. The fibers are cleaned and released from the digester as pulp.

Before the pulp can become paper, it must be bleached. After the bleaching process, the pulp is put into a papermaking machine. The machine mixes the pulp with water and sprays it onto a conveyor belt of mesh screens. These moving screens can travel at speeds ranging from 40 to 60 miles per hour. As the pulp moves on the conveyor belt, the water drains away leaving behind fibers that have bonded together and formed paper. The paper then goes through heated rollers that squeeze out the remaining water. Finally, the paper is wound into a giant roll where it can be cut and used for a variety of different products.

Styles of Music

Hans Christian Andersen, author of such fairytales as *The Little Mermaid* and *The Ugly Duckling,* once said, "Where words fail, music speaks." Music is a universal language that expresses thoughts, ideas, and emotions. It has the power to shape our attitudes and feelings. Music can make us dance or make us cry. Its sounds can be light and playful or heavy and solemn. Whatever its tone, music tells a story. How you hear that story, through its rhythms, melodies, or lyrics, is shaped by the musician's musical style. Here are four styles of music – jazz, rock and roll, country, and classical – and some of the musicians who made them popular:

Jazz music is a uniquely American creation. It developed in New Orleans in the early 1900s and combined elements of African sound, European band music, and American gospel. Jazz is known for its improvisational style and a rhythmic pattern with unusual and unexpected beats. There are several different types of jazz, including Dixieland, fusion, and soul. Legendary jazz figures include singer Billie Holiday and bandleader Duke Ellington.

Rock and Roll is a relatively young musical genre that also originated in the United States. In the 1950s, artists such as Chuck Berry and Elvis Presley blended various musical styles, including jazz, rhythm and blues, gospel, and country, to create the rock and roll sound. By the 1960s, rock music had an international flavor thanks to the "British Invasion," which featured such revolutionary bands as the Beatles and the Rolling Stones. Today, the term "rock music" encompasses a wide spectrum of musical sounds, including punk, heavy metal, grunge, and pop.

Country music originated in the American South and evolved from a popular regional style known as "folk" or "hillbilly." Country music is known for its honest and emotional lyrics that often relate to rural life, relationships, and faith. Instruments commonly associated with this genre include the fiddle, banjo, guitar, and harmonica. Legendary country musicians include the Carter Family, Hank Williams, Patsy Cline, Johnny Cash, Willie Nelson, and Loretta Lynn.

Classical music refers to a style of European music from the 18th and early 19th centuries. Sometimes referred to as "art music," this musical genre is often associated with concert halls, orchestras, and operas. Composers from that period include Ludwig Von Beethoven and Wolfgang Amadeus Mozart. Mozart wrote more than 40 symphonies during his life, and his most famous operas include *Don Giovanni* and *The Marriage of Figaro.* Beethoven was also a prolific composer and one of his most celebrated works is *Moonlight Sonata.*

The Color Wheel

Sir Isaac Newton developed the first color wheel in 1666. A color wheel is a circular diagram that depicts primary, secondary, and tertiary colors. Each color is positioned on the wheel according to its relationship to the other colors. Artists, graphic designers, interior decorators, and painters use color wheels to see the relationships between colors and how different color combinations can create the look or message they desire.

Most color wheels feature 12 colors. There are three primary colors (red, blue, and yellow), three secondary colors (purple, green, and orange), and six tertiary colors (red-violet, blue-violet, blue-green, yellow-green, yellow-orange, and red-orange). Primary colors are unique because they are used to create all other colors. However, no combination of other colors can create a primary color. Secondary colors are created by mixing two primary colors together in equal amounts. For example, combining yellow and blue makes green and mixing yellow and red creates orange. Tertiary colors result from mixing a primary color with a secondary color.

Colors that are side by side on a color wheel are related. They share a common color, such as the red in red-violet, red, and red-orange. Visually, colors that are related communicate a sense of harmony and order.

Colors that are opposite from each other on a color wheel are called complementary. They do not share a common color, such as red and green. Complementary colors are used to show dramatic contrasts. An example would be a painting of a green frog hopping on a red, sandy beach.

The Seven (or Six) Continents

The major landmasses of the world, typically separated from each other by bodies of water, are called continents. Most students in the United States learn about these seven: Africa, Antarctica, Asia, Australia/Oceania, Europe, North America, and South America. In other parts of the world, however, students learn about six continents because North America and South America are seen as the single continent, "America." Here are brief descriptions of the seven continents:

- Africa is the second largest continent. The Nile, the world's longest river, is found there. Approximately 840 million people live in Africa, which is comprised of more than 50 nations. Much of Africa is blessed with abundant natural resources, beautiful landscapes, and exotic wildlife. Yet many regions also are overwhelmed by famine, disease, civil unrest, and poverty.

- Antarctica is the coldest, driest, and southernmost of all the continents. Nearly all of Antarctica is covered by ice, and there is no native population. It's estimated that fewer than 200,000 people have ever been there. Most were scientists studying the continent's unique ecosystem, as well as global climate change.

- Asia is the world's largest continent, with more than 17 million square miles. It's also the most populated; three out of every five people on the planet live there. Asia stretches from the Middle East, and countries such as Saudi Arabia and Iraq, to the Far East, including the nations of Japan and China.

- Australia/Oceania is the world's smallest continent and includes Australia, New Zealand, New Guinea, and the South Pacific Islands. The vast majority of Australia's roughly 20 million residents reside in urban coastal areas. After Antarctica, it is the least populated continent on the planet.

- Europe is home to approximately 800 million people and comprises more than 40 nations. The largest is Russia and the smallest is Vatican City. The Ural Mountains are considered by many to be the geographical landmark separating Europe from the continent of Asia.

- North America is home to more than 20 nations, including the United States, Canada, and Mexico. The continent stretches northward from the Central American country of Panama to the Arctic and includes Greenland, the world's largest island.

- South America is home to the world's largest rainforest, the Amazon. The Amazon covers approximately 40 percent of the continent. South America connects to North America at the Isthmus of Panama, a narrow landmass that separates the Pacific Ocean from the Caribbean Sea.

The Sport of Polo

The word "polo" comes from the Tibetan word "pulu," which means ball. The sport of polo is considered one of the world's oldest organized games, dating back more than 2,000 years.

Played outdoors or indoors, polo is a contest of agility and endurance. In a polo match, two teams of four players (three if played indoors) are mounted on horseback. The objective is to score as many goals as possible by moving the polo ball downfield and through the opponent's goal posts. The team with the most goals at the end of the match wins.

Players hit the ball with a long-handled wooden mallet, which must be held in the right hand at all times. When struck with the mallet, the hard plastic ball can travel more than 100 miles per hour. The horses (also called polo ponies) can gallop at speeds approaching 40 miles per hour.

Polo matches have seven-minute time periods called "chukkers." Typically, there are six chukkers in a match, and after each one, players must change horses. This gives the tired horses a chance to rest. That means each team needs as many as 24 horses per match.

Play begins when the umpire rolls the ball onto the field (called a throw in) at the start of each chukker and after each goal. At halftime, spectators are encouraged to walk on the playing field and take part in a ritual known as "divot stomping." This involves stepping down on turf that has been torn up by the horses' hooves.

A regulation outdoor polo field is 300 yards long and 160 yards wide, which is equivalent to 10 acres or nine football fields. Arena polo (indoors) is played on a field that is 300 feet long and 150 feet wide. There are approximately 250 polo clubs and schools in the United States.

Venomous Snakes

There are four types of venomous snakes found in the United States – rattlesnakes, coral snakes, copperheads, and cottonmouths (also known as water moccasins). Venomous snakes use their fangs to bite and inject toxic saliva (venom) into their prey. The venom paralyzes the prey, allowing the snakes to kill, swallow, and digest their victims. All snakes are carnivores, and their diets can include insects, small rodents, birds, eggs, frogs, as well as other snakes. Here are brief descriptions of four venomous snakes:

Rattlesnakes are found in North and South America. In the United States, the largest concentration of rattlers is in the southwestern states, including Arizona and New Mexico. Rattlesnakes are sometimes called pit vipers because they have a heat-sensitive organ or "pit" on each side of their head that helps them locate prey. They also have a rattle, or interlocking beads at the tip of their tale, that makes a hissing sound when it vibrates. This sound is made to scare off predators. Rattlesnakes can swim, too. Some have been seen floating in water several miles from the nearest shoreline.

Coral snakes are known for their distinctive appearance. Their bodies feature circular bands or stripes of black, red, and yellow color. There are about 65 different species of coral snakes in the world, but only two are found in the United States – the eastern coral snake and the Arizona coral snake. Coral snakes in the United States grow to an average length of 24 inches. They spend much of their time underground or hidden underneath foliage, logs, and rocks.

Copperhead snakes are social snakes. It is common to find them hibernating in dens with other copperheads, or even other species of snakes. Their name reflects their appearance, which is a copper-colored head and reddish-brown body. Copperheads are found in the eastern and central United States and have a life span of about 18 years. Like the rattlesnake, copperheads use heat-sensitive pits to detect objects, like prey or predators, that are warmer than the surrounding environment.

Cottonmouths snakes are also called water moccasins because they are semiaquatic, meaning they live near water, including streams, ponds, lakes, and swamplands. The name cottonmouth comes from the snake's habit of opening its mouth wide, exposing the cotton-white tissue and lining inside. Cottonmouths often bare their fangs when they are alarmed or defensive. Their average size is between 30 and 48 inches long, and their lifespan is unknown.

Section 2

Summarizing Strategies

When students master the fundamentals of note taking, they can put more effort and concentration into synthesizing, rewording, and reorganizing content. Teaching students how to select and condense important facts and key details builds on the skills taught in the previous note-taking lessons, and sets students up for greater success in the classroom. Research shows that students who receive instruction in both note taking and summarizing can improve their academic performance by more than 30 percent.[1]

Summarizing information is a skill that involves the "comprehension, evaluation, condensation, and frequent transformation of ideas."[2] We want students to understand how to reduce information yet still capture the material's essence and essential meaning. Unfortunately, too many stumble in their attempts to either comprehend, evaluate, or condense information that's critical to their academic achievement.

The following lesson plans are designed to strengthen students' abilities to summarize information effectively and improve their analytical and critical-thinking skills. Students will learn how to identify main ideas, distinguish key facts from supporting details, paraphrase information, recognize and use introductory and closing statements, spot transition words and phrases, break down multiple ideas to see similarities and differences, and separate objective facts from subjective opinions.

---

1 Marzano, R.J., Pickering, D.J., & Pollock, J.E. (2001). **Classroom instruction that works.** Alexandria, VA: Association for Supervision and Curriculum Development.

2 Hidi, S., & Anderson, V. (1986). Producing written summaries: Task demands, cognitive operations, and implications for instruction. **Review of Educational Research, 56** (4), 473-493.

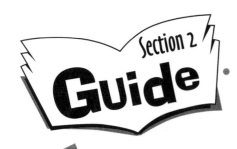

Section 2

Guide

Summarizing Lessons

Understanding Topics and Main Ideas

OBJECTIVE

Students will be able to differentiate between topics and main ideas in printed text.

MATERIALS

Overhead or LCD projector

Overheads
Topics and Main Ideas
Mother Nature

Worksheets (one per student)
Topics and Main Ideas
Mother Nature
'Perfect' Body

Answer Key Overheads
Mother Nature
'Perfect' Body

APPROXIMATE TIME

30 minutes

Introduction

- **G**ain students' attention.
- **R**eview key details from the most recent lesson (if applicable).
- Clearly state the **O**bjective of the lesson:
  - □ "Knowing the difference between topics and main ideas is an important first step in summarizing. In today's lesson, we are going to practice identifying topics and main ideas by reading a series of short articles."
- Explain **W**hy students should learn the information.
  - □ Explain to students that this summarizing skill can help them distinguish a topic from its main ideas. Point out that a topic is the big issue or concept being discussed and the main ideas relate to the topic.
  - □ Write the following topics on an overhead or the board: Extending the School Day, Mandatory Drug Testing for Student Athletes, and Requiring Uniforms in Public Schools. Ask students to think about each of these topics, and then call on students to share their thoughts. Write down their responses, and discuss how their answers can be used as main ideas. (Copy and save students' answers to use as a review exercise in Lesson 12: Identifying Supporting Details.)

Teacher Input/Modeling

- Use direct instruction to define topics and main ideas.
  - □ Use the Topics and Main Ideas overhead to explain the differences between topics and main ideas. Reveal each heading and subhead on the overhead one at a time, and have students follow along by completing their Topics and Main Ideas worksheet (distributed earlier). Periodically ask questions to check for understanding.

Guided/Independent Practice

- Follow up with a guided-practice exercise. Depending on students' understanding and skill level, do this exercise as a class or in small groups.

  □ Distribute copies of the Mother Nature worksheet. Instruct students to read the paragraph silently (taking no more than two minutes). As a class or in groups, have students answer the questions on the worksheet. Call on individuals (or groups) to share their answers. Record responses on the Mother Nature overhead as you go, and refer to the Mother Nature Answer Key overhead to show students other possible answers.

- Have students work independently to identify topics and main ideas.

  □ Distribute copies of the 'Perfect' Body worksheet. Instruct students to read the paragraph and then answer all of the questions. You can do this exercise during the lesson (if time allows) or assign it as homework.

Closure/Review

- Use the 'Perfect' Body Answer Key overhead to review students' worksheets, either at the end of the lesson or the following day. Ask students to share their answers aloud, before revealing the answers written on the overhead.

- At the end of the lesson, have students turn to a partner and explain the differences between topics and main ideas or verbally quiz students on how to identify main ideas.

Connection/Extension

- This lesson introduces a fundamental summarizing skill and can be connected to other summarizing skills, such as identifying supporting details and separating facts from opinions.

Topics and Main Ideas

I. **Topics**
    A. The general point being discussed
    B. Objective (factual; not influenced by emotions or biases)
    C. Who or what is the author discussing?

II. **Main Ideas**
    A. The author's point
    B. Subjective (biased; influenced by emotions or experience)
    C. Author's opinion
    D. What does the author believe about the topic?

III. **Identifying the Main Idea**
    A. Stated early in the reading
    B. Answers several key questions, but not necessarily all
        1. Who?
        2. What?
        3. When?
        4. Where?
        5. Why?
        6. How?
    C. *Thesis* and *theme* are synonyms for *main idea*

Topics and Main Ideas

Name: _____ Date: _____

I. Topics

    A.

    B.

    C.

II. Main Ideas

    A.

    B.

    C.

    D.

III. Identifying the Main Idea

    A.

    B.

        1.

        2.

        3.

        4.

        5.

        6.

    C.

Mother Nature

Name: _____ Date: _____

Have you ever watched *The Weather Channel*? If you have, then you know the amazing power of a tornado, a windstorm that can cause extensive destruction. Some powerful tornadoes have actually ripped houses off of their foundations and plucked cars right off the highway! The tornado is just one example of how nature can wreak havoc. Hurricanes also can cause extraordinary amounts of damage. Like tornadoes, hurricanes have tremendous winds, but with these winds come copious amounts of rain. Flooding often results. This flooding can leave people stranded in their homes and cars. These are two types of storms that can be devastating, and they can develop with little warning.

Who or what is this paragraph about (topic)?

What happened?

When?

Where?

How?

Why?

Topic:

Main Idea:

Mother Nature

(answers may vary)

Who or what is this paragraph about (topic)?
Tornadoes and hurricanes

What happened?
They can extensively damage our surroundings.

When? --

Where? --

How?
Their winds can ruin houses. Hurricanes can cause floods.

Why?
We don't often have a lot of warning and there is little we can do to prepare.

Topic:
Hurricanes and tornadoes

Main Idea:
Hurricanes and tornadoes are destructive forces of nature.

'Perfect' Body

Name: _____ Date: _____

Directions: *Read the following passage, and then answer the questions using the space provided.*

    Many people are familiar with the impact society has on the self-perceptions of adolescent girls. Too-thin models and celebrities create unhealthy body ideals that young American women strive to attain. In the United States, today's teenage boys feel similar anxiety about their physical appearance. Advertising bombards them with well-muscled, semi-clad young men. Like their female counterparts, teenage boys are afraid they cannot live up to the idealized image of their gender. Young men who are below (or above) average in height, weight, or both can suffer the most. Some react by exercising frequently and "bulking up." Others, convinced that no amount of physical exercise can help, withdraw from their peers to avoid teasing about their body size or shape. In both cases, resentment and anger can fester that create even more problems for these young men. While many school psychologists realize that male adolescents and teens are having severe body image problems, they are at a loss about how to solve the problem.

Who is the passage about?

What is happening?

When?

Where?

How?

Why?

What is the TOPIC of this paragraph? In other words, who is it about?

What is the MAIN IDEA of this paragraph? Combine your answers from above and write one sentence.

'Perfect' Body

(answers may vary)

Topics and Main Ideas

Who is the passage about?
Teenage boys

What is happening?
They're feeling anxious about their physical appearance.

When?
During their teen years

Where?
In the US

How?
They see advertising images that depict an unrealistic ideal. They find themselves not measuring up to these images.

Why?
Models and movie stars are not nearly the same as young teenage boys.

What is the TOPIC of this paragraph? In other words, who is it about?
Teenage boys

What is the MAIN IDEA of this paragraph? Combine your answers from above and write one sentence.
Teenage boys are becoming anxious about their physical appearance because of the unrealistic body images presented by male models.

Identifying Supporting Details

OBJECTIVE

Students will be able to identify supporting details and relate them to topics and main ideas in printed text.

MATERIALS

Overhead or LCD projector

Overheads
Defining Supporting Details
Oh Canada!

Worksheets (one per student)
Defining Supporting Details
Oh Canada!
Marine Life

Answer Key Overheads
Oh Canada!
Marine Life

APPROXIMATE TIME

30 minutes

Introduction

- **G**ain students' attention.
- **R**eview key details from the most recent lesson (if applicable).
  - ☐ If you recall from Lesson 11: Understanding Topics and Main Ideas, you were encouraged to save a copy of students' responses during a discussion on extending school days, mandatory drug testing, and requiring school uniforms. If available, display and review the answers given during that discussion. Ask students to define topics and main ideas, and then briefly discuss the importance of each.
- Clearly state the **O**bjective of the lesson:
  - ☐ "In today's lesson, we are going to define supporting details, including their function and where they are typically found, and then practice identifying supporting details by reading short articles."
- Explain **W**hy students should learn the information.
  - ☐ Explain to students that their ability to identify supporting information will allow them to better understand other people's perspectives. In addition, they need to use supporting details if they want to convince others that their ideas or opinions are valid and reasonable.
  - ☐ Tell students that it's not enough to just say what one thinks, but they must also tell why they think it. Explain how writers and lecturers use supporting details to argue their points of view and how readers and listeners also rely on supporting details to better understand why someone believes something.

Teacher Input/Modeling

- Use direct instruction to define and discuss supporting details.

□ Use the Defining Supporting Details overhead to explain how and why supporting details are used. Have students follow along by taking notes using their Defining Supporting Details worksheet (distributed earlier). Add any additional comments you deem necessary. Encourage student participation by periodically asking for feedback and checking for understanding.

Guided/Independent Practice

■ Follow up with a guided-practice exercise. Depending on students' understanding and skill level, do this exercise as a class or in small groups.

□ Distribute copies of the Oh Canada! worksheet. Instruct students to read the paragraph silently (taking no more than two minutes). As a class (or in groups) have students answer the questions on the worksheet. Call on individuals (or groups) to share their answers. Record responses on the Oh Canada! overhead as you go, and refer to the Oh Canada! Answer Key overhead to show students other possible answers.

■ Have students work independently to identify supporting details.

□ Distribute copies of the Marine Life worksheet. Instruct students to read the paragraph and then answer all of the questions. You can do this exercise during the lesson (if time allows) or assign it as homework.

Closure/Review

■ Use the Marine Life Answer Key overhead to review students' worksheets, either at the end of the lesson or the following day. Ask students to share their answers aloud, before revealing the answers written on the overhead.

■ At the end of the lesson, have students turn to a partner and discuss at least three examples of supporting details. Call on students to share their examples aloud.

Connection/Extension

■ If you feel your students are competent at identifying supporting details and knowing their purpose, move on to other summarizing lesson plans. If students need more practice mastering this skill, assign another reading assignment (from one of the articles on pages 90 - 103) and have students identify all of the supporting details.

Defining Supporting Details

I. **Supporting details**
    A. Come after the topic sentence (main idea)
    B. Make up the body of the paragraph

II. **Function of supporting details**
    A. Give details about main idea
    B. Support main idea

III. **Examples of supporting details**
    A. Facts
    B. Examples
    C. Statistics

IV. **Finding them while reading**
    A. Look in the middle of paragraphs
    B. Answer the "5 W's and H" questions

NOTE: Sub-details give specific information about the detail itself.

Name: _____ Date: _____

I.   **Supporting details**

    A.

    B.

II. **Function of supporting details**

    A.

    B.

III. **Examples of supporting details**

    A.

    B.

    C.

IV. **Finding them while reading**

    A.

    B.

NOTE: Sub-details give specific information about the detail itself.

Oh Canada!

Name: _____ Date: _____

There are three reasons why Canada is one of the best countries in the world. First, Canada has an excellent healthcare system. All Canadians have access to medical services at a reasonable price. Second, Canada has a high standard of education. Students are taught by well-trained teachers, and they're encouraged to continue their studies at universities. Finally, Canada's cities are clean and efficiently managed. Canadian cities have many parks and lots of space for people to live. All of these things make Canada a desirable place to live.

Topic:

Main Idea

Supporting details

1.

2.

3.

Sub-details

1. **All Canadians can get medical help pretty cheaply.**

2.

3.

Oh Canada!

(answers may vary)

Topic: Canada

Main Idea: Canada is a great place to live.

Supporting details:

1. Excellent healthcare system

2. Good education

3. Clean cities

Sub-details:

1. All Canadians can get medical help pretty cheaply

2. Highly qualified teachers; students encouraged to go to college

3. Lots of parks and living spaces

Marine Life

Name: _____ Date: _____

Directions: *Read the following passage, and then answer the questions using the space provided.*

The coelacanth (pronounced SEE-la-kanth) is one of the most intriguing examples of marine life. The coelacanth was believed to be extinct for 65 million years until one was found in 1938. Its fins are limb-like and people even sometimes call it "old four-legs!" It fascinates scientists because it is the modern representative of a group of fish that swam in the seas before there were any back-boned animals on land. Another interesting fact about the coelacanth is that coelacanth eggs hatch inside the mother, which is an effective way of protecting the eggs. A drawback to this, though, is that the coelacanth does not produce many eggs and it has only a few offspring at a time, making it extremely rare and vulnerable to over-fishing. The coelacanth is an intriguing mystery to scientists, marine enthusiasts, and people in general.

What is the topic of this paragraph?

What is the main idea of this paragraph?

There are four details that support the main idea. Write them down using your own words:

1.

2.

3.

4.

One of the supporting details listed above has sub-details that provide more information. Circle it, and then write its sub-details in your own words:

Marine Life

(answers may vary)

What is the topic of this paragraph?

The coelacanth

What is the main idea of this paragraph?

The coelacanth is intriguing.

There are four details that support the main idea. Write them down using your own words:

1. Believed to be extinct

2. Limb-like limbs give it the nickname of "old four legs"

3. A living example of fish that predate dinosaurs

4. Eggs hatch in the mother

One of the supporting details listed above has sub-details that provide more information. Circle it, and then write its sub-details in your own words:

When eggs hatch in the female coelacanth [detail], the young offspring are protected. Unfortunately, this method of reproduction really limits the number of offspring born. Plus, if a pregnant coelacanth is captured, several are in danger.

Paraphrasing

OBJECTIVE

Students will be able to paraphrase information from printed text.

MATERIALS

Overhead or LCD projector

Overheads
Paraphrasing Guidelines
Submerged Vehicle

Worksheets (one per student)
Paraphrasing Guidelines
Submerged Vehicle
Approaching Dogs

Answer Key Overheads
Submerged Vehicle
Approaching Dogs

APPROXIMATE TIME

30 minutes

Introduction

- **G**ain students' attention.
- **R**eview key details from the most recent lesson (if applicable).
- Clearly state the **O**bjective of the lesson:
  - "In today's lesson, we are going to learn more about how to paraphrase. We are going to review what paraphrasing means, and then practice how to paraphrase by reading a series of short articles and restating the information."
- Explain **W**hy students should learn the information.
  - Briefly define paraphrasing as using one's own words to describe what someone else has said or written. Point out that writers and lecturers often paraphrase when citing another person's ideas or words so they don't always have to use direct quotes, which can sometimes be difficult and time consuming.

Teacher Input/Modeling

- Use direct instruction to introduce students to paraphrasing.
  - Use the Paraphrasing Guidelines overhead to teach students how to paraphrase and the differences between paraphrasing and summarizing. Reveal each heading and subhead on the overhead one at a time, and have students follow along by completing their Paraphrasing Guidelines worksheet (distributed earlier). Add any additional comments you deem necessary. Encourage student participation by periodically asking for feedback and checking for understanding.

Guided/Independent Practice

- Follow up with a guided-practice exercise. Depending on students' understanding and skill level, do this exercise as a class or in small groups.

    - Distribute copies of the Submerged Vehicle worksheet. Instruct students to read the paragraph silently (taking no more than two minutes), and then follow the directions on their worksheet. Call on individuals (or groups) to share their answers. Record responses on the Submerged Vehicle overhead as you go, and refer to the Submerged Vehicle Answer Key overhead to show students other possible answers.

- Have students work independently to complete a paraphrasing exercise.

    - Distribute copies of the Approaching Dogs worksheet. Review the directions with the class, and then instruct students to complete the exercise. You can do this activity during the lesson (if time allows) or assign it as homework.

Closure/Review

- Ask for volunteers to read their paraphrases aloud, either at the end of the lesson or as a review the next day. Use the Approaching Dogs Answer Key overhead to show students an example of what they could have written.

- At the end of the lesson, ask students to reflect on the "how to" of paraphrasing. Have each student choose three steps to paraphrasing that he or she considers to be the most important, and then have students compare their choices with a partner.

Connection/Extension

- If you know your students have mastered the skill of paraphrasing, move on to other lessons related to summarization. If students require additional practice, choose one of the articles on pages 90-103 and have students paraphrase the content.

Paraphrasing Guidelines

I. **A paraphrase**
    A. Your way of presenting someone else's information and ideas
    B. It's an effective way to vary your writing when combined with summarizing and quotations
    C. It's much more detailed than a summary
    D. It should be roughly the same length as the original

II. **How to paraphrase**
    A. Keep all of the important ideas mentioned in the original
    B. Try to maintain the length of the original
    C Don't change the original meaning
    D. Use different sentence structures
       1. Use synonyms
       2. Change the order of ideas
       3. Experiment with different sentence styles
          a. Break long sentences into shorter ones and combine short sentences into longer ones
          b. Start sentences using gerunds (verb + *ing*)
    E. Double check to make sure you've retained the original meaning
    F. Make sure you cite your original source

Paraphrasing Guidelines

Name: _____ Date: _____

I.   **A paraphrase**

    A.

    B.

    C.

    D.

II. **How to paraphrase**

    A.

    B.

    C

    D.

        1.
        2.
        3.
            a.
            b.

    E.

    F.

Submerged Vehicle

Name: _____ Date: _____

Directions: *Read the following passage, underline all of the steps you should follow to escape a sinking vehicle, and then write a paraphrase of the information in the space provided.*

Do you know what to do if your car goes underwater, and you're still inside? According to www.ehow.com, there are several steps you should follow. First, stay calm. If you can escape before the car submerges, do so. If you think you cannot get out, open a window. Opening a window allows the pressure inside the car to equal the pressure outside the car. If you wait until the car is submerged to try to open a window, you won't be able to because of the water pressure. If you can't open a window or if the window is electric, try to break the glass by kicking it or smashing something against it. If you aren't successful, take a deep breath and open the car door after the car is completely submerged. It's important to know that the end of the car housing the engine will sink faster because of its weight. This might cause your car to flip. Finally, remember a couple pieces of advice: Don't rely on an air bubble like you might have seen in the movies, and don't try to gather your valuables before escaping.

Paraphrase:

Submerged Vehicle

Do you know what to do if your car goes underwater, and you are still inside? According to www.ehow.com, there are several steps you should follow. First, <u>stay calm</u>. If you can <u>escape</u> before the car submerges, do so. If you think you cannot get out, <u>open a window</u>. Opening a window <u>allows the pressure inside the car to equal the pressure outside the car</u>. If you wait until the car is submerged to try to open a window, you won't be able to because of the water pressure. If you can't open a window or if the window is electric, try to <u>break the glass by kicking it or smashing something against it.</u> If you aren't successful, <u>take a deep breath and open the car door after the car is completely submerged.</u> <u>It's important to know that the end of the car housing the engine will sink faster because of its weight.</u> This might cause your car to flip. Finally, remember a couple pieces of advice: <u>Don't rely on an air bubble like you might have seen in the movies, and don't try to gather your valuables before escaping.</u>

Paraphrase:

If you end up trapped underwater in a car, www.ehow.com has some advice. First, try not to be frantic and immediately try to get out before the car is submerged. If you see that the car is starting to go under, open a window right away to get the pressure inside of the car to be the same as the pressure outside the car. If the window won't move, try to shatter the glass by either kicking it or pounding it with something inside the car. If you can't do that, try to remain calm. By now, the car is almost submerged. Take a deep breath, open the car door, and swim to safety. Keep in mind that the engine is quite heavy and might cause the car to flip. Finally, don't waste your time looking for air bubbles like you've seen in the movies and leave your valuables behind.

Approaching Dogs

Name: _____ Date: _____

Directions: *You were assigned to write an article about how to approach a dog you don't know. You went to your local Humane Society and found a "How To" guide that had six guidelines (listed below). Read the Humane Society's recommendations, and then paraphrase the guidelines in the space provided.*

How to Approach an Unknown Dog
(United States Humane Society)

1. Only approach a leashed animal.

2. Ask the owner's permission.

3. If the dog shows signs of aggression (barking, growling, snarling, holding ears erect or tight against the head, holding tail stiffly, maintaining a rigid stance, bristling the hair), ask the owner to tighten the leash and move slowly away in a sideways direction.

4. Squat or crouch in front of the dog, holding out your hand, and allow the dog to approach you before starting to pet the animal.

5. Avoid staring directly into the dog's eyes, as this may be seen as a challenge.

6. Avoid patting the dog's head because the dog might perceive this as aggressive.

_____

_____

_____

_____

_____

_____

_____

_____

Approaching Dogs

When people see dogs, many want to pet them. Unfortunately, this sometimes can result in dogs biting or even attacking. When approaching an unfamiliar dog, a person should consider the Humane Society's advice. First, people should only approach dogs that are on a leash, and the person should ask the dog's owner if it is okay to pet the dog. The person should observe the dog, too. If the dog looks aggressive and is doing anything like barking, growling, snarling, pinning its ears, holding its tail or body rigidly, or bristling its hair, the person should leave. If the person must leave, she or he should ask the owner to tighten the dog's leash, and then the person should walk away slowly in a sideways direction. If none of these things are noted and the dog's owner gives permission, the person should get down on the dog's level by crouching. Then, the person should hold out her or his hand and wait for the dog to approach. While the dog sniffs the person's hand, the person should avoid touching the dog's head or looking directly into the dog's eyes because these actions might be seen as aggressive by the dog.

Using Introductory and Closing Statements

OBJECTIVE

Students will be able to explain the purpose of using introductory and closing statements and will be able to write their own introductory and closing statements.

MATERIALS

Overhead or LCD projector

Overheads
Introductory and Closing Statements
Submerged Vehicle

Worksheets (one per student)
Introductory and Closing Statements
Writing Introductory and
    Closing Statements

Answer Key Overheads
Submerged Vehicle
Writing Introductory and
    Closing Statements

APPROXIMATE TIME

20 minutes

Introduction

- **G**ain students' attention.
- **R**eview key details from the most recent lesson (if applicable).
- Clearly state the **O**bjective of the lesson:
    - □ "Today's lesson is about introductory and closing statements. We are going to define what each of these statements mean, and then practice writing introductory and closing statements based on information found in short paragraphs."
- Explain **W**hy students should learn the information.
    - □ Explain to students that being able to recognize introductory and closing statements in written text can help them better comprehend the material. In their own writing, using an introductory statement provides direction for what they want to say and helps guide the reader. The closing statement helps to reinforce or clarify previous information for the reader.

Teacher Input/Modeling

- Use direct instruction to explain the guidelines for writing introductory and closing statements.
    - □ Use the Introductory and Closing Statements overhead to define and explain both statements. Have students follow along by taking notes using their Introductory and Closing Statements worksheet (distributed earlier). Add any additional comments you deem necessary. Encourage student participation by periodically asking for feedback and checking for understanding.

Guided/Independent Practice

- Follow up with a group exercise.

    - Using the Submerged Vehicle overhead, have students silently read the paragraph from the overhead. After all students are done reading, ask them to raise their hands if they think the paragraph can be altered to make it easier to understand (most hands should go up). Point out that even though the information is good, most readers would have trouble making sense of the paragraph. Ask students how an introductory statement could improve the paragraph (refer them back to their notes if they need help). Use the Submerged Vehicle Answer Key overhead to reveal an example of an introductory sentence. Ask students for other examples, and write those on the overhead.

    - After discussing potential introductory statements, ask students to give you examples of closing statements that summarize the paragraph. If they need help, reveal the example written on the answer key overhead. Wrap up the discussion by asking students how a reader and a writer can benefit when both statements are used.

- Have students write their own introductory and closing statements.

    - Distribute copies of the Writing Introductory and Closing Statements worksheet. Instruct students to read each paragraph, and then write an introductory and closing statement for each in the space provided.

Closure/Review

- Use the Writing Introductory and Closing Statements Answer Key overhead to review and discuss possible answers.

- Ask students how they felt, as readers, trying to understand the paragraphs. Ask them what difference, if any, adding an introductory and concluding statement made.

Connection/Extension

- If you feel students need more guided or independent practice, ask them to find three samples of their own writing. Have them pick one paragraph from each sample and determine if it contains introductory and closing statements. If the chosen paragraph has one or both elements, have students underline the sentence(s). If the paragraph lacks one or both statements, have students write an introductory and/or concluding statement for the paragraph.

- This lesson nicely complements the lesson on paraphrasing. You also can extend this lesson to a writing exercise on how to create an introductory paragraph and concluding paragraph for essays or book reports.

Introductory and Closing Statements

I. **Introductory Statements**
   A. Appear at the beginning of your paragraph
   B. Answer the question, "What will this paragraph discuss?"
   C. Avoid using "I" or "You"
   D. Do not include opinions
   E. Maintain a neutral tone

II. **Closing Statements**
   A. Appear at the end of your paragraph
   B. Answer the question, "What was the main idea of this paragraph?"
   C. Do not introduce anything new
   D. Complement the introductory statement in terms of content
      1. Avoid expressing your opinion
      2. Maintain a neutral tone
      3. Use different words and/or sentence structure than your introductory statement

Introductory and Closing Statements

WOrkSheeT

Name: _____ Date: _____

I. Introductory Statements

  A.

  B.

  C.

  D.

  E.

II. Concluding Statements

  A.

  B.

  C.

  D. Complement the introductory
      statement in terms of content
      1.

      2.

      3.

Submerged Vehicle

If you think you cannot get out, open a window. Opening a window allows the pressure inside the car to equal the pressure outside the car. If you wait until the car is submerged to try to open a window, you won't be able to because of the water pressure. If you can't open a window or if the window is electric, try to break the glass by kicking it or smashing something against it. If you aren't successful, take a deep breath and open the car door after the car is completely submerged. It's important to know that the end of the car housing the engine will sink faster because of its weight. This might cause your car to flip. Finally, remember a couple pieces of advice: Don't rely on an air bubble like you might have seen in the movies, and don't try to gather your valuables before escaping.

Submerged Vehicle

(answers may vary)

Introductory Statement:
Knowing how to escape a submerged vehicle can save your life.

Concluding Statement:
A person in a submerged car is certainly in grave danger, but knowing what to do can mean survival.

Writing Introductory and Closing Statements

Name: _____ Date: _____

Directions: *Read the following paragraphs, and then write an introductory and closing statement for each in the space provided.*

1. According to experts, physical expressions will be limited and stiff, and the person will avoid making eye contact. While a deceitful person might touch his or her face, nose, and throat, this individual is unlikely to touch his or her heart with an open hand. You can also see if someone is faking emotions. Sometimes, gestures won't match the statement, and facial expressions will be limited to the muscles around the mouth instead of the whole face. Finally, verbal context and content might help identify lies. Many liars don't use contractions ("I was not there" as opposed to "I wasn't there). Liars might also talk too much, adding too many details because they aren't comfortable with silence. They might speak with a flat tone.

Introductory Statement:

Closing Statement:

2. Many skiers make escape plans when they arrive and look for protected areas. Experienced skiers also know that when they cross avalanche terrain, their group should be spread out because if an avalanche starts, chances are not everyone will get caught. If you see an avalanche starting, shout to make everyone aware of the danger. Get rid of all of your equipment so you can start "swimming" on the snow to stay on the surface. As you feel the snow begin to slow, try to make your way to the top (if you're underneath). Don't do this until it begins to slow, though, because you'll just waste energy and make little progress. Spend that energy keeping the snow out of your mouth and nose. When the snow slows, dig a space in front of you for air. Don't bother shouting for help – snow is a great sound-insulator and you want to conserve your energy.

Introductory Statement:

Closing Statement:

Writing Introductory and Closing Statements

(answers may vary)

Paragraph 1:

Introductory Statement:
It can be very helpful to know if the person you're talking to is telling the truth or feeding you a lie.

Closing Statement:
Recognizing the signs of deceit will enable you to know if the person you're talking to is trustworthy or not.

Paragraph 2:

Introductory Statement:
Avalanches don't happen often, but when they do, it's important to be prepared.

Closing Statement:
Knowing what to do when an avalanche strikes could save your life.

Using Transitions

OBJECTIVE

Students will be able to identify common transition words and phrases and use them to improve their writing skills.

MATERIALS

Overhead or LCD projector

Overheads
Defining Transitions
Choosing Transitions

Worksheets (one per student)
Defining Transitions
Common Transitions Study Guide
Choosing Transitions
Writing Transitions

Answer Key Overheads
Choosing Transitions
Writing Transitions

APPROXIMATE TIME

25 minutes

Introduction

- **G**ain students' attention.
- **R**eview key details from the most recent lesson (if applicable).
- Clearly state the **O**bjective of the lesson:
  - ☐ "In today's lesson, we are going to define what transitions are, learn common transition words and phrases, and practice identifying and writing transitions."
- Explain **W**hy students should learn the information.
  - ☐ Explain to students that transitions are helpful to both readers and writers. As a reader, a transition makes logical connections and helps you understand where the writer is going. As a writer, transitions make your writing better by making it more cohesive and coherent.

Teacher Input/Modeling

- Use direct instruction to introduce students to transitions.
  - ☐ Use the Defining Transitions overhead to explain and define transitions. Reveal each heading and subhead on the overhead one at a time, and have students follow along by taking notes on their Defining Transitions worksheet (distributed earlier). Add any additional comments or guidelines you deem necessary. Encourage student participation by periodically asking for feedback and checking for understanding.
  - ☐ Distribute copies of the Common Transitions Study Guide when you start to discuss how to choose transitions (main topic II, subtopic B on your Defining Transitions overhead). Instruct students to keep the study guide in a folder or taped inside a notebook for easy access. Let students know that you do not expect them to memorize the list of transitions, nor is it a

141

comprehensive list. Encourage students to write down other examples of transitions on their study guide whenever they learn new ones.

Guided/Independent Practice

■ Follow up with a guided-practice exercise. Depending on students' understanding and skill level, do this exercise as a class or in small groups.

   ☐ Distribute copies of the Choosing Transitions worksheet, and then use the Choosing Transitions overhead to lead the guided practice. Complete the first transition example for students and model your cognitive approach. You might describe your thought process like this:

> "I didn't eat all of my dinner. I was hungry by bedtime. When I think about how those two statements are related, I think that not eating all of my dinner CAUSED [verbal emphasis] my hunger. Looking at the Common Transitions Study Guide [refer students to the guide], I see there are transition words that indicate a consequence or result.

> "But notice that not all of them SOUND right. Even though they all can be used to indicate cause, they don't all work for these two sentences. The word or connector that sounds best is the word 'because.' It sounds right when you say aloud, 'I was hungry by bedtime because I didn't eat all my dinner.'

> "Did you notice how I changed the order of the words? That's okay as long as you keep the original meaning of the sentences."

   ☐ Once the activity is complete, call on individual students (or groups) for responses, before revealing the answers written on the Choosing Transitions Answer Key overhead.

■ Have students work independently to identify appropriate connectors and write transitions.

   ☐ Distribute copies of the Writing Transitions worksheet. Instruct students to read the directions, and then answer the questions using the space provided. You can do this exercise during the lesson (if time allows) or assign it as homework.

Closure/Review

■ Use the Writing Transitions Answer Key overhead to review students' worksheets, either at the end of the lesson or the following day. Ask students to share their answers aloud, before revealing the answers written on the overhead.

■ At the end of the lesson, have students turn to a partner and say as many transition words or phrases as they remember from each of the categories. Call on several students to answer aloud.

Connection/Extension

■ This activity complements the lesson on introductory and closing statements because both teach students how to focus their writing, making it more coherent and cohesive.

■ If students require additional practice, you can extend the lesson by choosing one of the articles on pages 90-103 and having students identify any transition words or phrases in the copy.

Defining Transitions

I. **Transitions**
   A. Words or phrases used to connect ideas
   B. Effective within a paragraph
   C. Especially important in longer writings when moving to a new paragraph

II. **Choosing a transition**
   A. Identify the relationship between the ideas you need to connect
   B. Choose a transition corresponding to the relationship
   C. Reread to make sure that the transition makes sense

Defining Transitions

Name: _____ Date: _____

I. Transitions

A.

B.

C.

II. Choosing a transition

A.

B.

C.

Common Transitions

Illustration: thus, for example, for instance, namely, to illustrate, in other words, in particular, specifically, such as

Addition: and, in addition to, furthermore, moreover, also, next, not only – but also, likewise, similarly, in the same way, for example, for instance, therefore

Time: after, afterward, next, last, at last, first, second, etc., rarely, usually, finally, at the same time, in the meantime, previously, immediately, eventually, later

Space: on top, over, along the edge, below, under, at the top, surrounding, at the rear, at the front, in front of, beside, behind, in the distance, beyond, across, adjacent, in the background

Concession: although, at any rate, at least, still, though, even though, while it may be true, in spite of, despite

Comparison: similarly, likewise, in like fashion, in the same manner, in like manner, once again

Contrast: on the contrary, but, however, nevertheless, despite, in contrast, yet, on one hand, on the other hand, while this may be true, even so

Emphasis: above all, indeed, truly, of course, certainly, surely, in fact, really, in truth, in addition, also

Examples: for example, for instance, to illustrate, thus, in other words, in particular

Consequence or Result: thus, consequently, hence, accordingly, for this reason, therefore, so, because, since, due to, as a result, in other words, then

Summary: therefore, finally, consequently, thus, in conclusion, as a result, accordingly

Choosing Transitions

Name: _____ Date: _____

I didn't eat all of my dinner. I was hungry by bedtime.

What is the relationship?

According to the Transitions Study Guide, what are my options based on the relationship type?

How can I combine these two sentences into a single sentence?

I am now healthy. I went to the hospital.

What is the relationship?

According to the Transitions Study Guide, what are my options based on the relationship type?

How can I combine these two sentences into a single sentence?

I studied for hours. I failed the English test.

What is the relationship?

According to the Transitions Study Guide, what are my options based on the relationship type?

How can I combine these two sentences into a single sentence?

I studied for hours. I aced the English test.

What is the relationship?

According to the Transitions Study Guide, what are my options based on the relationship type?

How can I combine these two sentences into a single sentence?

Choosing Transitions

(answers may vary)

I didn't eat all of my dinner. I was hungry by bedtime.

What is the relationship?
Consequence

According to the Transitions Study Guide, what are my options based on the relationship type?
thus, as a result, hence, because

How can I combine these two sentences into a single sentence?
I was hungry by bedtime because I didn't eat all my dinner.

I am now healthy. I went to the hospital.

What is the relationship?
Consequence

According to the Transitions Study Guide, what are my options based on the relationship type?
because

How can I combine these two sentences into a single sentence?
I am now healthy because I went to the hospital.

I studied for hours. I failed the English test.

What is the relationship?
Concession

According to the Transitions Study Guide, what are my options based on the relationship type?
despite, even though

How can I combine these two sentences into a single sentence?
I failed the English test even though I studied for hours.

I studied for hours. I aced the English test.

What is the relationship?
Consequence

According to the Transitions Study Guide, what are my options based on the relationship type?
because, as a result

How can I combine these two sentences into a single sentence?
Because I studied for hours, I aced the English test.

Lesson 15: Answer Key Overhead

Writing Transitions

Name: _____ Date: _____

Directions: *Read each sentence, and then circle the transition word or phrase that best belongs in the blank space.*

Circle the best connecting word:

1. The director explained that while the company certainly appreciates the work of its employees, the company did not require such a large workforce. _____ (Nevertheless, In other words, Similarly), people were getting fired.

2. Jefferson High School's basketball team is improving slowly. _____ (In comparison, Furthermore, With reference to), Roosevelt has won the last five games they've played.

3. To reduce people using cell phones while driving, some cities have recently made it illegal to talk while driving, _____ (in addition, as well as, in the same way as) imposing strict fines upon those who do.

4. Homework must be handed in on time, _____ (thus, or else, consequently) it will not be marked.

Directions: *Read the two sentences in each example, and then combine them into a single sentence using the most appropriate transition word or phrase. Refer to your study guide for help.*

1. *Cognates* are words that are spelled exactly or almost exactly the same in two languages. Radio is a Spanish cognate.

2. Geometry is difficult for me. I try to do the problems anyway.

3. Tony Blair is the most popular prime minister this century. Some people don't like him.

4. I found out I received a raise. I worked less.

5. Everyone wanted a new iPhone. They are so expensive.

6. Alligators have a broader, more rounded snout. Crocodiles have a narrower, more pointed snout.

Writing Transitions

Directions: *Read each sentence, and then circle the transition word or phrase that best belongs in the blank space.*

Circle the best connecting word:

1. The director explained that while the company certainly appreciates the work of its employees, the company did not require such a large workforce. _____ (Nevertheless, **In other words,** Similarly), people were getting fired.

2. Jefferson High School's basketball team is improving slowly. _____ (**In comparison,** Furthermore, With reference to), Roosevelt has won the last five games they've played.

3. To reduce people using cell phones while driving, some cities have recently made it illegal to talk while driving, _____ (in addition, **as well as,** in the same way as) imposing strict fines upon those who do.

4. Homework must be handed in on time, _____ (thus, **or else,** consequently) it will not be marked.

Directions: *Read the two sentences in each example, and then combine them into a single sentence using the most appropriate transition word or phrase. Refer to your study guide for help.*

1. *Cognates* are words that are spelled exactly or almost exactly the same in two languages. Radio is a Spanish cognate.
Cognates are words that are spelled exactly or almost exactly the same in two languages, such as radio which is a Spanish cognate.

2. Geometry is difficult for me. I try to do the problems anyway.
Geometry is difficult for me, but I try to do the problems anyway.

3. Tony Blair is the most popular prime minister this century. Some people don't like him.
Even though some people don't like Tony Blair, he is the most popular prime minister this century.

4. I found out I received a raise. I worked less.
Even though I received a raise, I worked less.

5. Everyone wanted a new iPhone. They are so expensive.
iPhones are so expensive, nevertheless everyone wants one.

6. Alligators have a broader, more rounded snout. Crocodiles have a narrower, more pointed snout.
Alligators have a broader, more rounded snout while crocodiles have a narrower, more pointed snout.

Lesson 15: Answer Key Overhead

Understanding Compare and Contrast

OBJECTIVE

Students will be able to organize information to help them compare and contrast two or more objects.

MATERIALS

Overhead or LCD projector

Overheads
Compare and Contrast Chart
How to Compare and Contrast

Worksheets (one per student)
How to Compare and Contrast
Compare and Contrast
    Independent Practice

APPROXIMATE TIME

30 minutes

Introduction

- **G**ain students' attention.

- Review key details from the most recent lesson (if applicable).

- Clearly state the **O**bjective of the lesson:
  - □ "In today's lesson, we are going to create compare and contrast charts so we can organize information based on the similarities and differences between two objects."

- Explain **W**hy students should learn the information.

  - □ Explain to students that when they compare and contrast two or more subjects, they need to be organized and thorough. Their thoughts have to be organized so they know what traits or facts belong to each subject, and how they are similar or different from the traits or facts of the other subjects. Students also need to be thorough, identifying as many factors or elements as possible so they will be able to judge how subjects are similar or different from one another.

Teacher Input/Modeling

- Use direct instruction to introduce the concept of comparing and contrasting.

  - □ Ask students to think about a situation in which they had to compare two issues or items (products, cars, sports teams, musicians, or other things appropriate and relevant to their age and skill level). Ask volunteers to describe the method they used to compare and contrast the two subjects or issues they chose. (Did they compare size, sound, price, color, weight, appearance, team records, etc.?) Write down students' examples on the board, and then choose one that will be easy to use as you further explain comparing and contrasting.

☐ Use the blank Compare and Contrast Chart overhead to model the process of comparing and contrasting by filling in the chart with information from the student example you chose. In the top left and top right column, write the names of the two things that were compared. In the center column, write all the factors or elements that the student considered when comparing and contrasting the two subjects (color, size, team records, weight, etc.). Here is an example of what the chart might look like if the comparison was between a Honda Accord and a Ford Focus:

Honda Accord		Ford Focus
	Cost	
	Mileage	
	Safety Rating	
	Color Choices	

☐ When you're done filling in the chart, explain to students that whether they are comparing and contrasting people, places, products, or ideas, it's a skill that many of them are already doing in their everyday lives.

☐ Continue direct instruction using the How to Compare and Contrast overhead. Explain one strategy for organizing information when reading text or writing a compare and contrast essay. Reveal each heading and subhead on the overhead one at a time, and have students follow along by taking notes using their How to Compare and Contrast worksheet (distributed earlier). Add any additional comments you deem necessary. Encourage student participation by periodically asking for feedback and checking for understanding.

Guided/Independent Practice

■ Follow up the discussion with a guided-practice exercise.

☐ Call on students to provide information for each of the blank spaces on the Compare and Contrast Chart at the bottom of the overhead and worksheet. (Although this can be an opportunity to practice research skills, the lesson is designed to reinforce students' organizational skills. The focus is on structure, not content. Answers should be realistic – not necessarily factual). When the chart is filled out, ask students what vehicle they would choose, using the "proof" listed on the chart.

■ Have students work independently to create and complete a compare and contrast chart using the information provided. Then, have students write a brief summary based on the information in their chart.

  ☐ Distribute copies of the Compare and Contrast Independent Practice worksheet. Instruct students to follow the directions and complete the exercise using the space provided on the worksheet. You can do this exercise during the lesson (if time allows) or assign it as homework

Closure/Review

■ Review students' worksheets to see if they completed their compare and contrast charts correctly. Discuss each scenario in class, and ask for volunteers to write their charts on the board and read their summaries aloud.

■ To summarize the lesson, explain how helpful a compare and contrast chart can be when a lecture or reading has two or more main subjects.

Connection/Extension

■ You can reinforce this lesson by doing a second exercise using guided or independent practice. You also can extend the lesson by having a discussion or doing an activity on how to create a planning sheet or outline prior to writing essays and reports.

Compare and
Contrast Chart

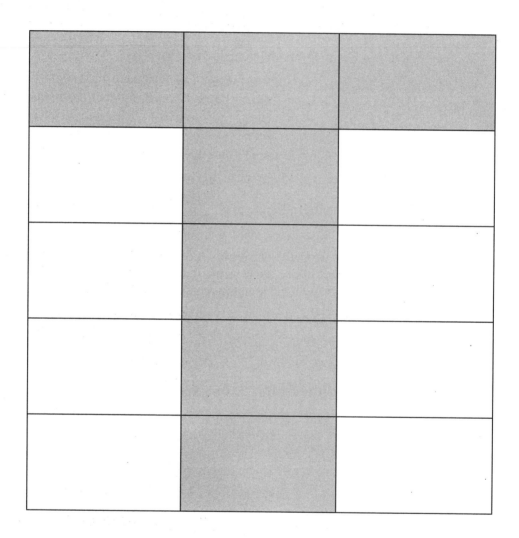

How to Compare and Contrast

I. **Being Prepared**

A. Expect to write compare and contrast essays in a range of academic courses, including English, history, geography, science, and art. Also, tests and quizzes often include compare and contrast essays and questions.

B. As a reader, look for signal words that indicate a writer is making a comparison or a distinction ("compare," "contrast," "alike," "similarities," and "differences")

II. **Organizing Information: An essential pre-writing task**

A. Make sure that the same characteristic is compared/contrasted for all subjects (when applicable).

B. Use a basic compare and contrast chart for two subjects.

C. Extend or enhance the compare and contrast chart when you have more than two subjects (see example).

···▶
How to Compare and Contrast (continued)

    D. Brainstorm as many characteristics as possible – some may not be "researchable."

    E. Fill in the compare and contrast chart as you brainstorm/research.

        1. View this as a work in progress.

        2. Add characteristics that you may have overlooked, and discard characteristics that seem too trivial.

	Honda Accord	Chevy Tahoe	Ford Focus
Cost			
Mileage			
Safety Rating			
Color Choices			

How to Compare and Contrast

Name: _____ Date: _____

I. Being Prepared
    A.

    B.

II. Organizing Information: An essential pre-writing task
    A.

    B.

    C.

    D.

    E.

        1.

        2.

	Honda Accord	Chevy Tahoe	Ford Focus
Cost			
Mileage			
Safety Rating			
Color Choices			

Lesson 16: Worksheet
©2008, Father Flanagan's Boys' Home

157

Compare and Contrast Independent Practice

Name: _____ Date: _____

Directions: *Read the following scenarios, and then choose one. Create a chart that compares and contrasts the two subjects or issues discussed in the scenario. After creating a compare and contrast chart, write a brief summary (one or two sentences) in which you list similarities and differences between the two topics. At the end of your summary, state what choice you would make and why.*

Your favorite music group is coming to town, but tickets are likely to cost close to $100. You would also like to buy some new accessories for your iPod, but you only have enough money to buy either the ticket or the accessories. Which one do you choose?

You and your friend are very Internet savvy. You disagree about which search engine is better – Google or Yahoo.

You are about to graduate, but you've not decided what you want to do. You know that you can either go to college full-time or go to work full-time. Which do you choose?

You are going on your summer vacation, but you don't know how to get there. Choose at least two types of transportation.

You're thinking about moving to a different community, one that you visited once. Compare and contrast the new community to your current hometown.

Separating Facts and Opinions

OBJECTIVE

Students will be able to distinguish statements of fact from statements of opinion in printed text.

MATERIALS

Overhead or LCD projector

Overhead
Separating Facts and Opinions

Worksheets (one per student)
Separating Facts and Opinions
Iowa Football
Fact, Opinion or Both?

Answer Key Overheads
Iowa Football
Fact, Opinion or Both?

APPROXIMATE TIME

40 minutes

Introduction

- **G**ain students' attention.
- **R**eview key details from the most recent lesson (if applicable).
- Clearly state the **O**bjective of the lesson:
  - □ "In today's lesson, we are going to define the differences between statements of fact and statements of opinion, and then practice identifying examples of each by reading a short article and brief statements."
- Explain **W**hy students should learn the information.
  - □ Explain to students that knowing the difference between facts and opinions will help them become more critical readers and better writers. As readers, it's important for them to recognize whether or not they are reading a subjective opinion or an objective fact. As writers, there are many times when they will need to present just the facts, rather than personal opinions or beliefs.

Teacher Input/Modeling

- Use direct instruction to explain the difference between facts and opinions.
  - □ Use the Separating Facts and Opinions overhead to teach students the difference between the two. Reveal each heading and subhead on the overhead one at a time, and have students follow along by taking notes on their Separating Facts and Opinions worksheet (distributed earlier). Add any additional comments or guidelines you deem necessary. Encourage student participation by periodically asking for feedback and checking for understanding.

Guided/Independent Practice

- Follow up with a guided-practice exercise. Depending on students' understanding and skill level, do this exercise as a class or in small groups.

  □ Distribute copies of the Iowa Football worksheet. Instruct students to read the paragraph silently (taking no more than one minute). As a class or in groups, find two sentences that are statements of opinion and two that are statements of fact. Call on individuals (or groups) for answers. Use the Iowa Football Answer Key overhead to provide students with other possible answers, if necessary.

- Have students work independently to identify facts and opinions.

  □ Distribute copies of the Fact, Opinion or Both? worksheet. Instruct students to read each sentence and decide if the statement is fact, opinion, or a combination of both. (Please note that number 4 includes several sentences, and students should classify each.) You can do this exercise during the lesson (if time allows) or assign it as homework.

Closure/Review

- Use the Fact, Opinion or Both? Answer Key overhead to review students' worksheets, either at the end of the lesson or the following day. Ask students to share their answers aloud, before revealing the answers written on the overhead.

- At the end of the lesson, have students turn to a partner and describe how a statement of fact differs from a statement of opinion. Call on several students to share their answers aloud.

Connection/Extension

- If students require additional practice, have students read an article from a magazine or newspaper and label sentences or paragraphs as facts or opinions.

- You also can connect this lesson to activities that teach critical thinking skills, media analysis, and journalism.

Separating Facts and Opinions

I. **Definitions (from Webster's Dictionary)**

   A. Fact: Anything that is done or happens; anything actually existent; any statement strictly true; truth; reality

      1. Concrete

      2. Can be documented

   B. Opinion: Indicating a belief, view, sentiment, conception

II. **Separating facts from opinions**

   A. Be aware of *descriptive* words; many opinions use them

      1. Descriptive words = words whose meanings change depending on who you talk to

      2. "Bad" might mean something completely different, depending on who you ask

   B. Watch out for words that compare (adjectives, especially those with -est and -er endings)

   C. Look for the words "more" and "most" before adjectives

Separating Facts and Opinions (continued)

D. Use questioning strategies to help you decide if something is an opinion
   1. Does this tell a thought or feeling?
   2. Would the statement be true all of the time?

III. **Replacing opinions with facts**
   A. Identify the part of a statement that's clearly an opinion:
      *This school is the **best**.*
   B. Consider what being the best means (the best grades, the best classes, the best teachers, etc.)
   C. Substitute highly subjective word(s) with words that are more objective and provable:
      *This school is the **highest performing in the district**.*
   D. Look for a fact that supports your opinion:
      This school is the highest performing in the district because its students average 29 on the ACT exam.

Separating Facts and Opinions

Name: _____ Date: _____

I. **Definitions (from Webster's Dictionary)**

    A. Fact: Anything that is done or happens; anything actually existent; any statement strictly true; truth; reality

        1.

        2.

    B. Opinion: Indicating a belief, view, sentiment, conception

II. **Separating facts from opinions**

    A. Be aware of *descriptive* words; many opinions use them

        1.

        2.

    B.

    C.

    D. Use questioning strategies to help you decide if something is an opinion

        1.

        2.

III. **Replacing opinions with facts**

    A.

    B.

    C.

    D.

Iowa Football

Name: _____ Date: _____

If you're a fan of college football, then your favorite team must be the Iowa Hawkeyes. Members of the Big Ten Conference, the Hawkeyes play their home games in historic Kinnick Stadium on the campus of the University of Iowa in Iowa City.

During football season, more than 70,000 Iowa fans pack the newly remodeled stadium to cheer on the Hawks. Obviously, Iowa fans are the best and most loyal. They create an electric atmosphere in and around the stadium on game days, which has to make fans of the opposing team jealous and insecure. Surely they know it will be nearly impossible for their team to win on Iowa's home field. This year, Iowa plays six of its 12 regular season games at Kinnick. Undoubtedly, they will go undefeated.

Identify two statements of fact:

1. _____

   _____

2. _____

   _____

Identify two statements of opinion:

1. _____

   _____

2. _____

   _____

Iowa Football

Facts: Members of the Big Ten Conference, the Hawkeyes play their home games in historic Kinnick Stadium on the campus of the University of Iowa in Iowa City.

This year, Iowa plays six of 12 regular season games at Kinnick.

During football season, more than 70,000 Iowa fans pack the newly remodeled stadium to cheer on the Hawks.

Opinions: If you're a fan of college football, then your favorite team must be the Iowa Hawkeyes.

Obviously, Iowa fans are the best and most loyal.

Surely they know it will be nearly impossible for their team to win on Iowa's home field.

Undoubtedly, they will go undefeated.

Fact, Opinion or Both?

Name: _____ Date: _____

Directions: *Read each statement and decide if it is a fact, opinion, or a combination of the two. Write your answer in the space provided below each sentence. If you label a sentence as an opinion, circle the word(s) that led to that decision.*

1. Schools should spend more money educating students.

2. You have the prettiest brown eyes.

3. In 2005, the District of Columbia spent approximately $16,000 per student.

4. Everyone loves the story of Ben Franklin's famous kite flight.

    Although he made many discoveries, Ben did not "invent" electricity.

    He did, however, invent the lightning rod, a device that protects buildings and other structures from lightning damage.

5. My country is not ready for a female president.

6. As of 2008, the United States has not had a female president.

7. It is easiest to go to the grocery store in the middle of the night.

8. If you don't like crowds, it is best to visit the grocery store in the middle of the night because there will usually be fewer people there.

Fact, Opinion or Both?

1. Schools **should spend** more money educating students. (opinion)

2. You have the **prettiest** brown eyes. (opinion)

3. In 2005, the District of Columbia spent approximately $16,000 per student. (fact)

4. **Everyone** loves the story of Ben Franklin's famous kite flight. (opinion)

   Although he made many discoveries, Ben did not "invent" electricity. (fact)

   He did, however, invent the lightning rod, a device that protects buildings and other structures from lightning damage. (fact)

5. My country **is not ready** for a female president. (opinion)

6. As of 2008, the United States has not had a female president. (fact)

7. It is **easiest** to go to the grocery store in the middle of the night. (opinion)

8. If you don't like crowds, **it is best** to visit the grocery store in the middle of the night because there will usually be fewer people there. (opinion and fact)

Writing a Summary

OBJECTIVE

Students will be able to distinguish between various types of summaries and will practice writing summaries of articles.

MATERIALS

Overhead or LCD projector

Overheads
Menu Summary
Movie Summary
Novel Summary
Guidelines for Writing a Summary
Choosing the Best Summary

Worksheets (one per student)
Spiders
Astronaut Sally Ride

Answer Key Overhead
Choosing the Best Summary

APPROXIMATE TIME

30 – 45 minutes or
two 20-minute sessions

Introduction

- **G**ain students' attention.
- **R**eview key details from lessons 2 (Note-Taking Guidelines), 11 (Understanding Topics and Main Ideas), and 12 (Identifying Supporting Details), and explain how using these skills can help students write better summaries.
- Clearly state the **O**bjective of the lesson:
  - □ "Authors use summaries to gain the interest and attention of their audience or to recap important details or themes. Summaries can provide readers with a preview of the content they are about to read or provide a review of key facts and information. A good summary simplifies and shortens an original work or text. In today's lesson, we are going to discuss how to write summaries. Then you will read an article and practice summarizing the information in your own words."
- Explain **W**hy students should learn the information.
  - □ Explain to students how summaries serve different purposes, depending on the context.
- Show students the Menu Summary overhead, and ask them if they ever read a menu item's description before deciding what to order.
- Show students the Movie Summary overhead, and ask them if they ever read movie reviews before choosing which film to see.
- Show students the Novel Summary overhead, and ask them if they ever read a book's synopsis, or back cover copy, to decide if they wanted to read the entire story.
  - □ Tell students that these are all examples of summaries, and each one helps the reader better understand the information and make more informed decisions. Remind students that a writer uses summaries to highlight main ideas and a reader uses summaries to

get a better grasp of the content. Point out that a good summary includes main ideas and details, but doesn't provide too much information.

Teacher Input/Modeling

■ Use direct instruction to teach the five steps to writing an effective summary.

  ☐ Use the Guidelines for Writing a Summary overhead to explain how to write a good summary. Have students take out a sheet of paper and take notes as you review the guidelines. Explain that an effective summary starts with an introductory sentence that states the main idea and then is followed by key facts and details listed in the order they appear in the original text.

Guided/Independent Practice

■ Follow up with a guided-practice exercise.

  ☐ Show students the Choosing the Best Summary overhead. Instruct them to silently read the paragraph from the overhead, decide which summary is the best, and state their choices aloud. Then reveal and explain the correct answer using the corresponding answer key overhead.

■ Do a second guided-practice activity.

  ☐ Distribute copies of the Spiders worksheet. As a group, read the spiders article aloud and underline or highlight the main ideas and key details. Have students write down the main ideas and details they identified, using the space provided at the bottom of their worksheet. Demonstrate for the students how the underlined or highlighted notes can be used to write a two- or three-sentence summary.

■ Have students work independently to summarize an article in their own words.

  ☐ Distribute copies of the Astronaut Sally Ride worksheet. Instruct students to read the directions and complete the exercise. Remind students to follow the guidelines for writing a summary when they summarize the article.

Closure/Review

- Ask students to share their summaries aloud. Discuss how their summaries are similar to or different from one you would have written.

- Summarize the lesson by reminding students that the skill of summarizing will help them better understand and remember information they read.

Connection/Extension

- To extend the lesson, ask students to write a summary or synopsis of a newspaper article or book they have recently read.

Menu Summary

Many restaurants include summaries on their menus to describe the dishes they offer and to entice customers to order certain foods.

Menu descriptions or summaries do not list **ALL** of the ingredients in a dish. For example, you would not see...

Double B.B.Q. Bacon Cheeseburger

1	pound lean ground beef
½	cup honey barbecue sauce, divided
¼	cup bread crumbs
4	1-ounce slices Swiss, Cheddar, or American cheese
4	slices of bacon, fried and drained
4	whole wheat hamburger buns, split
	Kosher salt and fresh ground pepper

Instead, menu descriptions or summaries are brief, precise, and describe only the most important and delicious aspects of an appetizer, entrée, or dessert...

Double B.B.Q. Bacon Cheeseburger

Our succulent double-decker cheeseburger is topped with crisp bacon and tangy barbecue sauce.

Summaries highlight the main elements or distinct features of a dish and give diners the basic information they need to make a choice.

Movie Summary

Movie summaries or synopses are written to provide readers or moviegoers with just enough information to make a decision about which films to see, or whether to see a movie at all.

When a movie summary or synopses is too long, some people may not take the time to read it and then decide to skip the movie. Others who read a long summary may feel it gave too much of the plot away and decide not to see the movie.

Here is an example of a movie summary that is too long:

The Museum of Natural History in New York City is the setting for this laugh-out-loud comedy starring America's favorite funnyman Ben Stiller. Stiller stars as Larry Daley, an unemployed, down-on-his-luck divorced dad. Needing to pay the bills, Larry takes a job as night watchman at the museum. On his first nightshift, Larry discovers this is not an ordinary job or museum.

As Larry strolls the hallways, he is shocked to see the exhibits come to life. The giant dinosaur skeleton at the museum's entrance steps off its pedestal and runs the hallways, chasing Larry and wreaking havoc. A statue of President Teddy Roosevelt (played to perfection by comic legend Robin Williams) and his horse comes to life, as does a whole army of miniature Roman soldiers and American cowboys. Larry can't believe his eyes or who he is bumping into, including Christopher Columbus (who Larry is slow to recognize), Attila the Hun, and Sacagawea.

Larry soon learns that an Egyptian artifact with magical powers is responsible for bringing all of the museum's inhabitants to life – but only between sundown and sunup, when the museum is closed. Three other night watchmen, played by veteran actors Dick Van Dyke, Mickey Rooney, and Bill Cobbs, know about the artifact's special powers. This trio of elderly guards attempts to steal the artifact from the museum and it's up to Larry and his museum "friends" to stop them. If they fail, all of the animals and exhibits will never come to life again.

Directed by Shawn Levy and based on the children's book by Milan Trenc, this film delivers action and laughs that will appeal to moviegoers of any age.

A better summary of this movie might be:

A newly hired night watchman at New York's Museum of Natural History experiences the shock of his life when he sees the museum's animals and exhibits spring to life.

Novel Summary

When authors write summaries of their novels, they highlight the plot and theme of their stories.

You will often see a summary about a book written on its back cover. This summary provides a brief overview of the content and helps readers decide if they want to read the entire story.

Here is an example of a novel summary:

The Freedom Writers Diary
by Erin Gruwell and the Freedom Writers

This 320-page paperback is a collection of diary entries written by high school students from the Los Angeles area. Each entry provides a glimpse into their lives and struggles, including gang violence, addictions, and homelessness. Despite such challenges, the students, with the help of a very determined teacher, find the strength and courage to overcome their hardships and achieve.

Guidelines for Writing a Summary

To write a summary, follow these steps:

1) **SKIM** the article or text to obtain a general understanding of the information it contains.

2) **REREAD** the entire article or text carefully, highlighting key words and phrases.

3) **TAKE NOTES** on the main ideas and the details that support them. As you take notes:

   a. Use your own words.

   b. State the main idea in the first sentence.

   c. Include only important information such as names, dates, places, etc.

   d. Keep the information in the order in which it is presented.

4) **WRITE THE SUMMARY** using information taken from your notes.

5) **EVALUATE YOUR SUMMARY** for appropriate length and content; include the most important information.

Choosing the Best Summary

Summarize this paragraph:

Bullies thrive in environments where adults are not present and where there is little help or support for victims. Cyberspace, or the online world, is such an environment. Almost any verbal, social, sexual, or emotional bullying that can be done face to face is being done online, often anonymously. Rumors are spread. Threats are made. Reputations are ruined. The ease and speed of the Internet allows bullies to taunt their victims again and again before an audience of thousands. Cyberbullies create Web sites and blogs to post ugly comments and unflattering pictures. They use e-mail to spread rumors and send cruel jokes. They use instant messaging to embarrass or exclude others. Even cell phones are used to send threats in the form of text-messages. The protective barriers of time and place that once shielded victims from constant torment no longer exist. Anyone, anywhere, at any time, can be victimized.

Choosing the Best Summary (continued)

Summary A:

Threats and rumors spread quickly on the Internet. Kids can gang up on others using instant messages, e-mails, blogs, cell phones, and other technology.

Summary B:

Bullies can attack their victims any time and any place because of the Internet. For instance, bullies use Web sites and blogs to make fun of others. They spread rumors using e-mail, and they make threats by sending text messages on cell phones. Bullies can attack their victims verbally, socially, sexually, or emotionally, and they can ruin other people's reputations. Bullies can get away with their attacks because bystanders don't intervene to help victims and adults are not present.

Summary C:

Cyberbullies are using the Internet and other technologies to threaten, harass, and humiliate their victims. The speed of the Web and the lack of adult supervision means bullies can spread rumors and make hateful comments quickly, anonymously, and constantly.

Choosing the Best Summary

Summary A:

Threats and rumors spread quickly on the Internet. Kids can gang up on others using instant messages, e-mails, blogs, cell phones, and other technology.

Answer: This is not the best summary. It is too brief and lacks critical details. For example, the word "bullies" or "cyberbullies" is not used. This summary does not capture the true meaning of the paragraph.

Summary B:

Bullies can attack their victims any time and any place because of the Internet. For instance, bullies use Web sites and blogs to make fun of others. They spread rumors using e-mail, and they make threats by sending text messages on cell phones. Bullies can attack their victims verbally, socially, sexually, or emotionally, and they can ruin other people's reputations. Bullies can get away with their attacks because bystanders don't intervene to help victims and adults are not present.

Answer: This is not the best summary. This summary includes too many details from the original paragraph and is almost as long. This summary should be shorter and focus on the main ideas.

Summary C:

Cyberbullies are using the Internet and other technologies to threaten, harass, and humiliate their victims. The speed of the Web and the lack of adult supervision means bullies can spread rumors and make hateful comments quickly, anonymously, and constantly.

Answer: Of the three summaries, this is the best. It is effective because it describes the main points, accurately captures the meaning of the paragraph, and does not include unimportant details.

Spiders

Name: _____ Date: _____

Perhaps one of the least known and most feared members of the animal kingdom is the spider. Because of this, spiders are often killed on sight. In reality, however, spiders are one of man's best friends. They kill thousands of insects each year, preventing the insects from destroying crops. Spiders also are useful because strands from the webs they weave can sometimes be used as cross ties in certain microscopes.

A spider's body consists of two parts. The first part is called the thorax. The posterior section is called the abdomen. Spiders possess four pairs of legs and mandibles, which are similar to jaws. They also have spinnerets located in the abdomen that they use to spin their webs.

There are several known types of spiders. The largest spider is the tarantula. The most dangerous spider is the black widow. The black widow's venom is toxic and has been known to cause death.

Write the main idea of this article:

_____

_____

List the important ideas and details the writer includes:

- _____
- _____
- _____
- _____
- _____

Create a summary by rewriting the main idea(s) and details in your own words:

_____

_____

_____

Astronaut Sally Ride

Name: _____   Date: _____

Directions: *Read the following biography, and then answer the questions using the space provided.*

"Neither of my parents were scientists, but that didn't matter. They encouraged me to explore the things that interested me. And they encouraged me to be curious, to ask questions, and to think about things for myself. All of these things helped me to become a scientist and an astronaut."

Astronaut. Author. American trailblazer. As the first American woman in space, Sally Ride ignited the imaginations of millions, most notably young girls.

A native of Southern California, Sally Kristen Ride was born on May 26, 1951. In her youth, she was an avid tennis player who dropped out of college for a short time to pursue a professional tennis career. Fearing her skill level would limit her success as a pro athlete, Ride decided her talents were better suited to science. She returned to college and earned several degrees, including a doctorate in physics from Stanford University.

In 1977, she applied to become a NASA astronaut after reading an advertisement in the university newspaper. The following year she was selected as an astronaut candidate and began a one-year training program, which involved parachute jumping, water survival, radio communications, and navigation training. She successfully completed the program and on June 18, 1983, she boarded the space shuttle Challenger as a mission specialist. She and four other astronauts spent 147 hours in space before returning to Earth on June 24. A year later, Ride was aboard the Challenger for a second space flight. During that eight-day mission, the crew conducted scientific experiments and deployed a satellite.

In 1986, America's space program suffered a significant setback when the Challenger exploded during liftoff. At the time, Ride was preparing for a third space mission. However, the accident led NASA to temporarily suspend its training program. Ride was then appointed to a special Presidential Commission that investigated the cause of the explosion. She retired from NASA in 1987 and returned to Stanford University to be a Science Fellow at the Center for International Security and Arms Control.

Today, Ride is an advocate for science education and is involved in a variety of projects that encourage girls to pursue careers in math, science, and technology. Ride has authored several science books for children and has received numerous accolades, including induction into the National Women's Hall of Fame and the Astronaut Hall of Fame.

In your own words, write the main idea of this article:

_____

_____

_____

In your own words, list the important ideas and details presented in the article:

- ■ _____
- ■ _____
- ■ _____
- ■ _____
- ■ _____
- ■ _____
- ■ _____
- ■ _____
- ■ _____
- ■ _____

In your own words, summarize the article in one paragraph:

_____

_____

_____

_____

_____

_____

_____

Research Strategies

The digital age has transformed the way many of our students search for and find information. Whether they're researching facts about the government of Uruguay or describing the paintings of Caravaggio, students seem to prefer surfing the Web over browsing a reference book. While that's understandable, and perhaps in some situations preferable, the ease of the Internet does not eliminate one fundamental problem many students have: a lack of basic research skills.

Students who do not know how to use, nor understand the value of, encyclopedias, almanacs, and even dictionaries are going to struggle doing research online and off. In our experience, students need instruction in a variety of areas. We've had students who didn't know reference books used guide words, what guide words did, or where to find them. We've watched students spend countless hours searching through encyclopedias because they

never bothered to look at the index, or simply didn't know that the content was alphabetized. Some still struggled even after being told the content was in alphabetical order. We've seen students grab dictionaries to find antonyms and open thesauruses to find definitions. And when it comes to the Internet, we've heard some students say they use Wikipedia for all of their research material while others complained the Internet overwhelmed them with information they didn't want or understand.

The following lessons are designed to empower students with fundamental skills to do basic research better. There are lessons to help students use a range of reference materials, including encyclopedias, thesauruses, and almanacs. There also is a lesson plan aimed at teaching students how to refine their online search strategies so they won't get swamped with unnecessary and unreliable information.

Section 3

Guide

Research Lessons

LESSON 19

Using Different References

OBJECTIVE

Students will be able to identify a variety of reference materials and explain which ones are most useful when doing different types of research.

MATERIALS

Overhead or LCD projector
Reference books
  (atlas, almanac, dictionary, encyclopedia, thesaurus, etc.)

Overhead

Types of References

Worksheets (one per student)

Types of References
Which Reference Book Is Best?
Almanac, Atlas or Thesaurus?

Answer Key Overheads

Which Reference Book Is Best?
Almanac, Atlas or Thesaurus?

APPROXIMATE TIME

20 minutes

Introduction

- **G**ain students' attention.
- **R**eview key details from the most recent lesson (if applicable).
- Clearly state the **O**bjective of the lesson:
  - □ "In today's lesson, we are going to review the types of information, such as facts and statistics, that are found in different reference books and materials."
- Explain **W**hy students should learn the information.
  - □ Explain to students that reference books serve different purposes. Some, such as almanacs, can provide statistical information related to specific years or geographic locations. Other reference books, such as encyclopedias or biographical dictionaries, provide detailed information about people, places, and things. The more familiar students are with the kinds of information available in different reference books, the more efficient their research efforts will be when searching for answers and information.

Teacher Input/Modeling

- Use direct instruction to explain the content contained in various reference books.
  - □ Display a variety of research books, and then ask students to think about which one(s), if any, they have used and for what purpose. Ask for volunteers to share their experiences. After a brief discussion, distribute copies of the Types of References worksheet. Have students take notes on their worksheet as you define and explain each reference written on the Types of References overhead. Encourage participation by asking students to define each reference before revealing the descriptions written on the overhead. Add any

additional comments or reference materials you deem necessary, and periodically ask for feedback and check for understanding.

Guided/Independent Practice

■ Follow up with a group exercise. Depending on students' understanding and skill level, do this exercise as a class or in small groups.

  ☐ Explain to students that you will ask them a series of questions. After each question, have them tell you the research tool (from their Types of References worksheet) that will be most helpful for finding the answer. Call on individual students (or groups) for responses and then discuss. Several suggested questions are listed below, or you may choose to ask about issues or subjects that your students are currently studying.

   ☐ Who was Martin Luther King?
     (Biographical Dictionary/Encyclopedia)

   ☐ What was the population of Sacramento, California, in 2002?
     (Almanac)

   ☐ Who invented the cotton gin?
     (Biographical Dictionary/Encyclopedia)

   ☐ What is an antonym for the word "ridiculous"?
     (Thesaurus)

   ☐ Of the five Great Lakes, which is the smallest?
     (Atlas)

■ Have students work independently to identify the most useful reference book for finding answers to a variety of different questions.

  ☐ Distribute copies of the Which Reference Book Is Best? worksheet. Review the directions with the class, and then instruct students to complete the exercise. You can do this activity during the lesson (if time allows) or assign it as homework.

Closure/Review

■ Use the Which Reference Book Is Best? Answer Key overhead to review students' worksheets, either at the end of the lesson or the next day. Ask students to share their answers aloud, before revealing the answers written on the overhead.

■ To summarize the lesson, ask students to discuss the differences between a dictionary and thesaurus and the differences between a biographical dictionary and encyclopedia.

Connection/Extension

■ If you feel students need additional practice, a second worksheet and corresponding answer key (Almanac, Atlas or Thesaurus?) are provided.

■ This lesson is a natural lead in to other research skills, such as using guide words, encyclopedias, and almanacs. You also can connect this lesson to any academic task that requires students to find specific facts or data.

Types of References

Name: _____ Date: _____

Main Ideas/ Keywords	Details/ Ex./ Definitions
Dictionary	
Thesaurus	
Encyclopedia	
Atlas	
Almanac	
Biographical Dictionary	
Internet	
Other	

Types of References

Main Ideas/ Keywords	Details/ Ex./ Definitions
Dictionary	Definitions, Pronunciations, Spelling Other forms of words Care → caring Extra information, such as currency charts
Thesaurus	Synonyms, Antonyms, Related words
Encyclopedia	Short essays on people, places, things (look up by last name)
Atlas	Places, Populations, Landmarks
Almanac	Data (number of people living in Rhode Island who have a college degree) Statistics (Wyoming has the smallest population of any state) Yearly awards (winner of the 2000 World Series, winner of the 1990 Nobel Peace Prize, etc.)
Biographical Dictionary	Information on famous people by categories, such as African Americans, women, etc. (look up by last name)
Internet	Just about everything Pros: current, all topics, immediate Cons: not always reliable, too much information, inefficient searches
Other	

Which Reference Book Is Best?

Name: _____ Date: _____

Directions: *Read each question, and then choose a reference from the list that you think is the best source for finding the answer.*

References: Almanac, Atlas, Biographical Dictionary, Encyclopedia, Thesaurus

1. What were the results of the 1968 presidential election?
    Reference book: _____

2. What was the route of the Lewis and Clark expedition?
    Reference book: _____

3. What is the name of the award given annually for outstanding achievement in physics, chemistry, literature, economics, medicine, and peace?
    Reference book: _____

4. What are the major rivers of Asia?
    Reference book: _____

5. Who in this list was not an inventor?
    a. Thomas Edison
    b. J. Edgar Hoover
    c. Eli Whitney
    d. Alexander Graham Bell
    Reference book: _____

6. How many planetary satellites are in our solar system?
    Reference book: _____

7. How many Great Lakes are there, and what are their names?
    Reference book: _____

8. In 2000, what was the average rainfall in the state of South Carolina?
    Reference book: _____

9. What year was Benjamin Franklin born?
    Reference book: _____

10. What are three words that mean the same thing as "friendly"?
    Reference book: _____

Which Reference Book Is Best?

1. What were the results of the 1968 presidential election?
   Reference book: _____ *Almanac* _____

2. What was the route of the Lewis and Clark expedition?
   Reference book: _____ *Atlas or Encyclopedia* _____

3. What is the name of the award given annually for outstanding achievement in physics, chemistry, literature, economics, medicine, and peace?
   Reference book: _____ *Almanac* _____

4. What are the major rivers of Asia?
   Reference book: _____ *Atlas* _____

5. Who in this list was not an inventor?
   a. Thomas Edison
   b. J. Edgar Hoover
   c. Eli Whitney
   d. Alexander Graham Bell
   Reference book: _____ *Encyclopedia or Biographical Dictionary* _____

6. How many planetary satellites are in our solar system?
   Reference book: _____ *Almanac* _____

7. How many Great Lakes are there, and what are their names?
   Reference book: _____ *Atlas* _____

8. In 2000, what was the average rainfall in the state of South Carolina?
   Reference book: _____ *Almanac* _____

9. What year was Benjamin Franklin born?
   Reference book: _____ *Encyclopedia or Biographical Dictionary* _____

10. What are three words that mean the same thing as "friendly"?
    Reference book: _____ *Thesaurus* _____

Lesson 19: Answer Key Overhead

Almanac, Atlas or Thesaurus?

WORkShEeT

Name: _____ Date: _____

Directions: *Read each statement, and then choose the reference that is the most appropriate for finding the answer. Write the corresponding letter for your answer in the space provided.*

A. Almanac   B. Atlas   C. Thesaurus

1. _____   A synonym for the word "tremendous"

2. _____   The shortest route for a plane to fly from Madrid, Spain to Paris, France

3. _____   The major rivers of Africa

4. _____   Presidential election results from 1988

5. _____   All the states that border Kansas

6. _____   Medal winners in basketball at the 2000 Summer Olympics

7. _____   An antonym for the word "disgrace"

8. _____   Average life expectancy for Japanese females

9. _____   The capital of Afghanistan

10. _____   The major cities of the world

Almanac, Atlas or Thesaurus?

A. Almanac   B. Atlas   C. Thesaurus

1. **C**   A synonym for the word "tremendous"

2. **B**   The shortest route for a plane to fly from Madrid, Spain to Paris, France

3. **B**   The major rivers of Africa

4. **A**   Presidential election results from 1988

5. **B**   All the states that border Kansas

6. **A**   Medal winners in basketball at the 2000 Summer Olympics

7. **C**   An antonym for the word "disgrace"

8. **A**   Average life expectancy for Japanese females

9. **B**   The capital of Afghanistan

10. **B**   The major cities of the world

Lesson 19: Answer Key Overhead

LESSON **20**

Understanding Alphabetization

OBJECTIVE

Students will be able to alphabetize a word list, including alphabetizing to the fourth letter or beyond.

MATERIALS

Overhead or LCD projector
Telephone directories

Worksheets (one per student)
Writing Words in Alphabetical Order
Alphabetizing Words

Answer Key Overheads
Writing Words in Alphabetical Order
Alphabetizing Words

APPROXIMATE TIME

20 minutes

Introduction

- **G**ain students' attention.
- **R**eview key details from the most recent lesson (if applicable).
- Clearly state the **O**bjective of the lesson:
  - □ "In today's lesson, we are going to practice alphabetization, including how to alphabetize words that have the first, second, and third letters in common."
- Explain **W**hy students should learn the information.
  - □ Explain to students that understanding how words and information are alphabetized in reference books makes the books easier to use and can shorten the length of time they spend searching for content. Point out how this skill applies to everyday activities, such as using a phone book to find the number of their favorite restaurant or finding a book in the school library.

Teacher Input/Modeling

- Use direct instruction to explain how words are alphabetized A to Z, and how it's sometimes necessary to look beyond the first letter to determine alphabetical order.
  - □ Distribute a phone directory to each student. If there are not enough for everyone, divide the students into groups and have each group share a directory. Ask students to find their last names in the directory, and then write the last name that comes before and after their own (and all like it). For example, a student whose last name is Cooper might write Coop (the name preceding all of the Cooper names) and Coopers (the name after the last Cooper entry). Ask for volunteers to write their three names vertically on the board or overhead. For example:
    Preceding name: Stumme
    Student's name: Stumo
    Following name: Stump

☐ At least one of the examples should have several identical letters at the beginning of each name. Explain to students that when they alphabetize, or need to find words and names in a directory or dictionary, they sometimes have to identify the first letter that is different in order to determine the alphabetical order.

Guided/Independent Practice

■ Guide students through an alphabetizing exercise.

☐ Choose words that have the first several letters in common but are not already in alphabetical order (unlike names in a phone directory). Here is an example:

Transportation
Transplant
Transfer
Trampoline
Tranquil

■ Have students work independently to alphabetize words.

☐ Distribute Writing Words in Alphabetical Order worksheets. Instruct students to review the words listed in the columns, and rewrite them in alphabetical order.

Closure/Review

■ Use the Writing Words in Alphabetical Order Answer Key overhead to review students' worksheets, either at the end of the lesson or the next day. Ask students to share their answers aloud, before revealing answers on the overhead.

■ At the end of the lesson, ask students to explain what they need to do if two or more words have the first, second, third, or fourth letters in common.

Connection/Extension

■ This lesson provides a nice introduction to other research skills, including how to use encyclopedias, almanacs, and thesauruses. You also can connect this lesson to any activity that teaches students about indexes, as they also are alphabetized.

■ If you feel students need additional guided or independent practice, do another exercise in class. A second activity worksheet and corresponding answer key (Alphabetizing Words) are provided, or have students create an alphabetized class roster by first or last name.

Writing Words in Alphabetical Order

Name: _____ Date: _____

Directions: *Write the words in each column in alphabetical order. Remember, when you have words that start with the same letter(s), look for the first different letter.*

A.   volleyball   _____

     basketball   _____

     football   _____

     soccer   _____

     wrestling   _____

     track   _____

B.   history   _____

     math   _____

     reading   _____

     science   _____

     English   _____

     music   _____

C.   space   _____

     straws   _____

     solar   _____

     steak   _____

     stray   _____

     spaghetti   _____

D.   translation   _____

     transfer   _____

     trance   _____

     tranquil   _____

     transmit   _____

     tribal   _____

A B C D E F G H I J K L M N O P Q R S T U V W X Y Z

Writing Words in Alphabetical Order

A. volleyball   _basketball_

   basketball   _football_

   football   _soccer_

   soccer   _track_

   wrestling   _volleyball_

   track   _wrestling_

B. history   _English_

   math   _history_

   reading   _math_

   science   _music_

   English   _reading_

   music   _science_

C. space   _solar_

   straws   _space_

   solar   _spaghetti_

   steak   _steak_

   stray   _straw_

   spaghetti   _stray_

D. translation   _trance_

   transfer   _tranquil_

   trance   _transfer_

   tranquil   _translation_

   transmit   _transmit_

   tribal   _tribal_

Alphabetizing Words

Name: _____ Date: _____

Directions: *Write the words in each column in alphabetical order. Remember, when you have words that start with the same letter(s), look for the first different letter.*

A. graphic   _____

    samples   _____

    illustrate   _____

    cowboys   _____

B. hatchback   _____

    heritage   _____

    honor   _____

    humble   _____

C. black   _____

    brave   _____

    bread   _____

    block   _____

D. token   _____

    total   _____

    tongue   _____

    tomato   _____

E. comic   _____

    compare   _____

    comma   _____

    comb   _____

Alphabetizing Words

A. graphic   _cowboy_

    samples   _graphic_

    illustrate   _illustrate_

    cowboys   _samples_

B. hatchback   _hatchback_

    heritage   _heritage_

    honor   _honor_

    humble   _humble_

C. black   _black_

    brave   _block_

    bread   _brave_

    block   _bread_

D. token   _token_

    total   _tomato_

    tongue   _tongue_

    tomato   _total_

E. comic   _comb_

    compare   _comic_

    comma   _comma_

    comb   _compare_

Using Guide Words

OBJECTIVE

Students will be able to use guide words when searching through reference books.

MATERIALS

Overhead or LCD projector

Overheads
Sample Dictionary Page
Guide Words: Fatal and Fearful

Worksheets (one per student)
Sample Dictionary Page
Using Guide Words

Answer Key Overhead
Using Guide Words

APPROXIMATE TIME

20 minutes

Introduction

- **G**ain students' attention.
- **R**eview key details from the most recent lesson (if applicable).
- Clearly state the **O**bjective of the lesson:
  - □ "In today's lesson, we will define guide words, their purpose, and how to use them when searching through encyclopedias, dictionaries, and other reference books."
- Explain **W**hy students should learn the information.
  - □ Explain to students that guide words can help them locate information more quickly. They can use guide words whenever they're looking up definitions or spellings in a dictionary, searching for names in a phone book or business directory, or trying to find a subject in an encyclopedia.

Teacher Input/Modeling

- Use direct instruction to define "guide words."
  - □ The American Heritage Dictionary, for example, defines "guide word" as a "word or term that appears at the top of each page or column in a reference book, such as a dictionary, to indicate the first or last entry on the page."
  - □ Copy a page from a dictionary, and then convert it into an overhead. Make additional copies as hand outs for students. Using the overhead, show students the guide words. Explain that the word in the upper left corner represents the first word or entry on the page, and the guide word in the upper right corner represents the last word or entry on the page. Point out that all the entries or words listed on the page are in alphabetical order, and note any instances where words are alphabetized to the second, third, or fourth letter.

Guided/Independent Practice

- Follow up with a guided-practice exercise using the Fatal and Fearful overhead.

    □ Ask students to review the words written on the overhead, and then have them say aloud which ones they think would appear on a page that had fatal and fearful as the guide words. Put a check next to their answers. When they are done giving responses, review and discuss their choices, making any corrections necessary. End the exercise by asking students if the unchecked words (those that are not between fatal and fearful) would come before or after the page with those two guide words.

- Have students work independently to apply what they've learned about guide words.

    □ Distribute copies of the Using Guide Words worksheet. Review the directions with the class, and then instruct students to complete the exercise. You can do this activity during the lesson (if time allows) or assign it as homework.

Closure/Review

- At the end of the lesson, or as a review the following day, ask students to share their answers aloud before revealing the correct answers written on the Using Guide Words Answer Key overhead.

- To summarize the lesson, ask students what a guide word in the upper left corner signals compared to a guide word in the upper right corner. Call on students for answers.

Connection/Extension

- This lesson complements other research-related lessons, including using an encyclopedia, almanac, and thesaurus. You also can have students practice using guide words in any assignment related to alphabetizing words, looking up names in a directory, or finding definitions.

Guide Words:
fatal and fearful

fate _____   favor _____

fifty _____   fearful _____

fault _____   fasten _____

fear _____   faucet _____

Using Guide Words

Name: _____ Date: _____

Directions: *In the space provided, write YES or NO if you think the word would be on the same page as the two guide words written in bold.*

A. Guide words: **moccasin/molar**

_____ 1. mock

_____ 2. mode

_____ 3. motel

_____ 4. molecule

_____ 5. modest

_____ 6. model

_____ 7. modify

_____ 8. moat

_____ 9. moist

_____ 10. moment

B. Guide words: **process/professor**

_____ 1. produce

_____ 2. product

_____ 3. privilege

_____ 4. proclamation

_____ 5. promise

_____ 6. professor

_____ 7. proceed

_____ 8. proclaim

_____ 9. prize

_____ 10. propel

Using Guide Words

A. Guide words: **moccasin/molar**

Yes 1. mock

Yes 2. mode

_No_ 3. motel

_No_ 4. molecule

Yes 5. modest

Yes 6. model

Yes 7. modify

_No_ 8. moat

Yes 9. moist

_No_ 10. moment

B. Guide words: **process/professor**

Yes 1. produce

Yes 2. product

_No_ 3. privilege

Yes 4. proclamation

_No_ 5. promise

Yes 6. professor

_No_ 7. proceed

Yes 8. proclaim

_No_ 9. prize

_No_ 10. propel

Using a Thesaurus

OBJECTIVE

Students will know the purpose of a thesaurus, understand the information it contains, and demonstrate how a thesaurus can help them expand their vocabularies.

MATERIALS

Overhead or LCD projector
Thesauruses

Overheads
Sample Thesaurus Entry
Choosing the Best Synonyms
  and Antonyms

Worksheet (one per student)
Using a Thesaurus –
  Synonyms and Antonyms

Answer Key Overheads
Choosing the Best Synonyms
  and Antonyms
Using a Thesaurus –
  Synonyms and Antonyms

APPROXIMATE TIME

20 minutes

Introduction

- **G**ain students' attention.
- **R**eview key details from the most recent lesson (if applicable).
- Clearly state the **O**bjective of the lesson:
  - □ "Today's lesson is about how and when to use a thesaurus. We also are going to practice using a thesaurus to find synonyms and antonyms."
- Explain **W**hy students should learn the information.
  - □ Explain to students that the purpose of a thesaurus is to find synonyms for a word. This can help them avoid repeating the same word or phrases in their writing assignments. A thesaurus also can provide them with a word's antonym, or opposite. Point out that a thesaurus is a great tool for helping them expand their vocabularies and improve their writing skills.

Teacher Input/Modeling

- Use direct instruction to explain why and when students should use a thesaurus.
  - □ Use the Sample Thesaurus Entry overhead to explain the type of information students will find when looking up words in a thesaurus. Highlight the similarities between a dictionary and thesaurus, and explain to students that when they look for a word's synonyms, they shouldn't assume that every synonym will be an appropriate replacement because the context may be wrong or the meaning is slightly different. Remind students to use a dictionary in conjunction with a thesaurus when they want to use a word or phrase that is unfamiliar to them.

    ☐ Point out that the first entry on the overhead provides synonyms for the word "form," when it's used as a noun. Be sure to mention that the "(n)" is an abbreviation for noun. The second entry provides synonyms for the word "form," when it's used as a verb. Again, point out that the "(v)" is an abbreviation for verb. Also discuss how students can use the capitalized words inside the parentheses to find additional synonyms.

Guided/Independent Practice

■ Follow up with a guided-practice exercise.

    ☐ Use the Choosing the Best Synonyms and Antonyms overhead to highlight why some synonyms and antonyms don't work as replacement words. Read each sentence on the overhead aloud, and then ask students to identify which word (from the choices listed) is the most appropriate replacement for the word written in ALL CAPS. (A corresponding answer key is provided.)

■ Have students work independently to identify synonyms and antonyms.

    ☐ Distribute copies of the Using a Thesaurus – Synonyms and Antonyms worksheet. Review the directions with the class, and then instruct students to complete the exercise. You can do this activity during the lesson (if time allows) or assign it as homework.

Closure/Review

■ At the end of the lesson, or as a review the following day, ask students to share their answers aloud, before revealing the correct answers written on the Using a Thesaurus – Synonyms and Antonyms Answer Key overhead.

■ To summarize the lesson, lead a discussion with students about what they have learned about using a thesaurus.

Connection/Extension

■ This lesson complements any writing exercise designed to help students overcome the common problem of starting successive sentences and paragraphs with identical words and phrases.

Sample
Thesaurus Entry

Words in a thesaurus are listed alphabetically, just as they are in a dictionary. Here is an example of how the word "form" appears in a thesaurus:

form, n. manner, fashion, mode (METHOD); object, thing, phenomenon (VISION); embodiment, cast, conformation (SHAPE); bench, settle (SEAT); class, grade, room (LEARNING).

form, v. fabricate, organize, structure (MAKE-UP); compose make up, constitute (PART); fashion, forge, devise (PRODUCTION); mold, pat, whittle (SHAPE)

Source: Roget's New Pocket Thesaurus in Dictionary Form. Norman Lewis, Editor. Pocket Books, New York, N.Y. 1972. Page 168.

Choosing the Best Synonyms and Antonyms

Each sentence has one word written in ALL CAPS. Choose which SYNONYM is the most appropriate replacement for that word:

After the farm accident, Mr. Grey was very FRAIL.

dainty   *slight*   *weak*

Sean bullied everyone, but he was especially CRUEL to Kahlil.

vicious   *malignant*   *degenerate*

The citizens were tired of all the crime and violence, so they held a PEACE rally.

quiet   *tranquil*   *unity*

The dancers moved across the stage GRACEFULLY.

tastefully   *sweetly*   *elegantly*

Each sentence has one word written in ALL CAPS. Choose which ANTONYM is the most appropriate replacement for that word:

Dominic never studied, and he never turned in his homework. He was a DILIGENT student.

lazy   *heavy-footed*   *sluggish*

Candace was HONEST when she lied to her friends and family about what she had done.

double-dealing   *dishonest*   *counterfeit*

The family's pet cat eats five times a day, plus scraps from the dinner table, and is now extremely SKINNY.

lumpish   *roly-poly*   *fat*

The running back ran down the sidelines and no one could catch him because he was so SLOW.

hypersonic   *fleet*   *speedy*

Lesson 22: Overhead

210   ©2008, Father Flanagan's Boys' Home

Choosing the Best Synonyms and Antonyms

Each sentence has one word written in ALL CAPS. Choose which SYNONYM is the most appropriate replacement for that word:

After the farm accident, Mr. Grey was very **WEAK**.

Sean bullied everyone, but he was especially **VICIOUS** to Kahlil.

The citizens were tired of all the crime and violence, so they held a **UNITY** rally.

The dancers moved across the stage **ELEGANTLY**.

Each sentence has one word written in ALL CAPS. Choose which ANTONYM is the most appropriate replacement for that word:

Dominic never studied, and he never turned in his homework. He was a **LAZY** student.

Candace was **DISHONEST** when she lied to her friends and family about what she had done.

The family's pet cat eats five times a day, plus scraps from the dinner table, and is now extremely **FAT**.

The running back ran down the sidelines and no one could catch him because he was so **SPEEDY**.

Using a Thesaurus – Synonyms and Antonyms

Name: _____ Date: _____

Directions: *Using a thesaurus, read each question and then underline the correct answer(s).*

1. Which two words are synonyms for the word **archaic**?
   obsolete   old-fashioned   modern   unbearable

2. Which three words are synonyms for the word **resources**?
   assets   capital   expend   property

3. Which word is not a synonym for the word **devour**?
   guzzle   spend   consume   conserve

4. Which word is an antonym for the word **surreptitious**?
   atmosphere   stealth   brazen   dedication

5. Which three words are synonyms for the word **sling**?
   hurl   pitch   sneak   heave

6. Which word is an antonym for the word **torrid**?
   crime   artic   hinged   heated

7. Which three words are synonyms for the word **trinity**?
   trudge   trio   triune   troika

8. Which three words are synonyms for the word **disheveled**?
   scruffy   messy   tidy   rumpled

9. Which two words are antonyms for the word **diminish**?
   boost   diminish   dwindle   enlarge

10. Which three words are synonyms for the word **incompatible**?
    conflicting   discordant   discrepant   imaginable

Using a Thesaurus Synonyms and Antonyms

1. Which two words are synonyms for the word **archaic**?
   obsolete   **old-fashioned**   modern   unbearable

2. Which three words are synonyms for the word **resources**?
   assets   **capital**   expend   **property**

3. Which word is not a synonym for the word **devour**?
   guzzle   spend   consume   **conserve**

4. Which word is an antonym for the word **surreptitious**?
   atmosphere   stealth   **brazen**   dedication

5. Which three words are synonyms for the word **sling**?
   hurl   **pitch**   sneak   **heave**

6. Which word is an antonym for the word **torrid**?
   crime   **artic**   hinged   heated

7. Which three words are synonyms for the word **trinity**?
   trudge   **trio**   **triune**   **troika**

8. Which three words are synonyms for the word **disheveled**?
   scruffy   **messy**   tidy   **rumpled**

9. Which two words are antonyms for the word **diminish**?
   boost   diminish   dwindle   **enlarge**

10. Which three words are synonyms for the word **incompatible**?
    conflicting   **discordant**   **discrepant**   imaginable

Using an Encyclopedia

OBJECTIVE

Students will be able to use an encyclopedia to locate information and do research more quickly and accurately.

MATERIALS

Overhead or LCD projector
Encyclopedias

Worksheets (one per student)
The Encyclopedia
Independent Practice

Answer Key Overheads
The Encyclopedia
Independent Practice

APPROXIMATE TIME

20 minutes

Introduction

- **G**ain students' attention.
- **R**eview key details from the most recent lesson (if applicable).
- Clearly state the **O**bjective of the lesson:
  - ☐ "In today's lesson, we are going to review how an encyclopedia can be used to do research more effectively and efficiently."
- Explain **W**hy students should learn the information.
  - ☐ Explain to students that encyclopedias provide a wealth of accurate and detailed information that is useful when writing reports or studying for exams. Point out that content in an encyclopedia is organized alphabetically, and entries with lots of information often have their content divided into sections or subtopics that allow users to find specific facts and details more easily.

Teacher Input/Modeling

- Use direct instruction to describe how to use an encyclopedia effectively.
  - ☐ Give each student one volume of an encyclopedia and discuss its various sections. If there are not enough encyclopedias for everyone, divide the students into groups and have each group share one. Review the index, explaining that it's alphabetized to help readers locate specific topics and subtopics. Show students examples of guide words, and remind them of their purpose. Point out any examples where multiple subtopics or subheadings are used to organize related facts and information in entries that have lots of information.

Guided/Independent Practice

- Follow up with a guided-practice exercise to help students identify main topics or subjects that are searchable in an encyclopedia. Depending on students' understanding and skill level, do this exercise as a class or in small groups.

  □ Distribute copies of The Encyclopedia worksheet, and read the directions to the class. As a class or in groups, have students fill in the blanks on the worksheet. Call on individuals (or groups) to share their responses before revealing the correct answers written on The Encyclopedia Answer Key overhead.

- Have students work independently to identify appropriate search words and topics.

  □ Distribute copies of the Independent Practice worksheet. Review the directions with the class, and then instruct students to complete the exercise. You can do this activity during the lesson (if time allows) or assign it as homework.

Closure/Review

- Use the Independent Practice Answer Key overhead to review students' worksheets, either at the end of the lesson or the following day. Ask students to share their answers aloud, before revealing the answers written on the overhead.

- To summarize the lesson, ask students to explain why it's important to know what the main topic is before starting their research.

Connection/Extension

- This lesson provides students with a basic understanding of how to use an encyclopedia and complements any activity or exercise in which students have to present written or oral reports about people, places, or things.

The Encyclopedia

Name: _____ Date: _____

Directions: *Read each statement, and then decide what topic or subject you would search for in an encyclopedia to obtain additional information.*

When Cindy saw Italy on the map, she could not understand how farm products could be raised in a country that was a peninsula.

MAIN TOPIC: _____

POSSIBLE SUBTOPICS: _____

After reading a short story about Albert Einstein* and his theory of relativity, Thom wanted to learn more about the man and the theory. Thom grabbed his encyclopedia and searched for...

_____ and _____

* Remember, individuals are alphabetized by their last, not first, name.

Encyclopedia entries with large amounts of information are often divided into sections or subtopics. Read the subtopics under Sydney in the box below, and then answer the questions:

Sydney, Australia

Geographic Setting and Climate	Culture and Recreation	Government
Population	Education	Economy
Layout and Landmarks	Transportation	History

---

1. To find out how many universities are located in Sydney, which subtopic should you read? _____

2. Which subtopic would you want to read before packing your bags? _____

3. To learn more about the major manufacturing industries in Sydney, which subtopic should you read? _____

4. If you want to know who the first European visitor to the Sydney area was, which subtopic should you read? _____

The Encyclopedia

When Cindy saw Italy on the map, she could not understand how farm products could be raised in a country that was a peninsula.

MAIN TOPIC: _____ *ITALY* _____

POSSIBLE SUBTOPICS: _*FARM PRODUCTS; PENINSULA*___

After reading a short story about Albert Einstein* and his theory of relativity, Thom wanted to learn more about the man and the theory. Thom grabbed his encyclopedia and searched for...

_*EINSTEIN, ALBERT*___ and _*THEORY OF RELATIVITY.*___

* Remember, individuals are alphabetized by their last, not first, name.

> **Sydney, Australia**
> | Geographic Setting | Culture and Recreation | Government |
> | and Climate | Education | Economy |
> | Population | Transportation | History |
> | Layout and Landmarks | | |

1. To find out how many universities are located in Sydney, which subtopic should you read?

   _*EDUCATION*_____

2. Which subtopic would you want to read before packing your bags?

   *GEOGRAPHIC SETTING & CLIMATE*

3. To learn more about the major manufacturing industries in Sydney, which subtopic should you read?

   _*ECONOMY*_____

4. If you want to know who the first European visitor to the Sydney area was, which subtopic should you read?

   _*HISTORY*_____

Independent Practice

Name: _____ Date: _____

Directions: *Read each statement, and then decide what topic or subject you would search for in an encyclopedia to obtain additional information.*

Andrew was interested in raising tropical fish. He was given an aquarium for his birthday, but he wasn't sure if it was the best one for tropical fish. To find out, Andrew grabbed his encyclopedia and looked up _____ and _____.

Cameron has to explain why Americans pay taxes to the government. In the encyclopedia, Cameron searches under _____ to find a possible answer.

Jalen's assignment requires him to define fossil fuel and solar energy, explain how each is used, and then compare and contrast their advantages and disadvantages. He searched for _____ and _____ in his encyclopedia.

Joaquin is writing a biography of Abraham Lincoln based on historical sites and landmarks in Lincoln's home state of Illinois. He starts his research by looking up _____ and _____ in his encyclopedia.

Caden's teacher asks him to tell the class about Margaret Mead. Caden grabs his encyclopedia and looks up _____.

For English class, Keira has to write a short biography on the famous Nebraska writers, Willa Cather, Mari Sandoz, and John Neihardt. She starts her search by looking up _____ and _____ and _____ in the encyclopedia.

Independent Practice

Directions: *Read each statement, and then decide what topic or subject you would search for in an encyclopedia to obtain additional information.*

Andrew was interested in raising tropical fish. He was given an aquarium for his birthday, but he wasn't sure if it was the best one for tropical fish. To find out, Andrew grabbed his encyclopedia and looked up __*TROPICAL FISH*__ and __*AQUARIUM.*__ .

Cameron has to explain why Americans pay taxes to the government. In the encyclopedia, Cameron searches under __*TAXES*__ to find a possible answer.

Jalen's assignment requires him to define fossil fuel and solar energy, explain how each is used, and then compare and contrast their advantages and disadvantages. He searched for __*FOSSIL FUEL*__ and __*SOLAR ENERGY*__ in his encyclopedia.

Joaquin is writing a biography of Abraham Lincoln based on historical sites and landmarks in Lincoln's home state of Illinois. He starts his research by looking up __*LINCOLN, ABRAHAM*__ and __*ILLINOIS*__ in his encyclopedia.

Caden's teacher asks him to tell the class about Margaret Mead. Caden grabs his encyclopedia and looks up __*MEAD, MARGARET.*__ .

For English class, Keira has to write a short biography on the famous Nebraska writers, Willa Cather, Mari Sandoz, and John Neihardt. She starts her search by looking up __*CATHER, WILLA*__ and __*SANDOZ, MARI*__ and __*NEIHARDT, JOHN*__ in the encyclopedia.

Using an Almanac

OBJECTIVE

Students will be able to use an almanac to broaden their research skills, as well as their general knowledge.

MATERIAL

Overhead or LCD projector
Almanacs

Worksheet (one per student)
Using an Almanac

Answer Key Overhead
(design your own, depending on the almanac used)

APPROXIMATE TIME

20 minutes

Introduction

- **G**ain students' attention.
- **R**eview key details from the most recent lesson (if applicable).
- Clearly state the **O**bjective of the lesson:
  - ☐ "Today's lesson is about almanacs. We are going to learn why they are such a valuable research tool, and how almanacs can broaden your general knowledge and make your essays and reports more descriptive."
- Explain **W**hy students should learn the information.
  - ☐ Explain to students that almanacs provide unique and specialized information. Point out that sports trivia, election results, facts about countries, and descriptions of significant events are a few examples of what can be found in almanacs.

Teacher Input/Modeling

- Use direct instruction to show students what they can find in an almanac (facts about American states, territories, and cities; regional and global economic data; nations and flags of the world; Supreme Court decisions; Olympic medal winners; Oscar winners; etc.)
  - ☐ Give each student an almanac to browse. If there are not enough almanacs for everyone, divide students into groups and have each group share one. Call on students (or groups) to name one topic or subject listed in the index, and then have students turn to the appropriate page and read the information provided about that topic. Discuss how the information can be integrated into research reports and writing assignments.

Guided/Independent Practice

- Have students work independently to find information in an almanac. In order to review students' worksheets, students will need to complete the exercise using the same edition of the book (The 2001 World Almanac and Book of Facts, 2007 Time Almanac, etc.).

  □ Distribute copies of the Using an Almanac worksheet. Review the directions with the class, and then instruct students to complete the exercise.

  □ The worksheet in this lesson cites information from *The New York Times Almanac 2002* and *The World Almanac and Book of Facts 2007*. You may need to edit the worksheet, or create a completely new set of questions, to accurately reflect the content available in your almanac, as well as the age and skill level of your students.

Closure/Review

- At the end of the lesson, or the following day, ask students to share their answers aloud. Discuss how and when an almanac can be used to accomplish other academic tasks.

- To summarize the lesson, have students turn to a partner and discuss the different types of information available in almanacs.

Connection/Extension

- This lesson complements any exercise or assignment in which students need to provide data, statistics, or trivia.

- You also can tie this lesson to a creative writing exercise, and have students use an almanac to write essays that are more thorough and descriptive.

Using an Almanac

Name: _____ Date: _____

Directions: *Fill in the blanks with information found in your almanac. Please include the page number that your answer was found on.*

1. The Hispanic population in Chicago, Illinois, in 2000: _____ pg. _____

2. The average life expectancy for males living in Italy: _____ pg. _____

3. Who has the longer life expectancy in the United States, men or women? _____ pg. _____

4. The number of inmates on death row in Texas prisons: _____ pg. _____

5. The winner of the NBA (National Basketball Association) title in 1986: _____ pg. _____

6. The origins of the state name "Florida": _____ pg. _____

7. The median income for American females who do not have a high school diploma: _____ pg. _____

8. The number of soldiers in the Russian Army in 2000: _____ pg. _____

9. The number of households headed by unmarried couples in 1998: _____ pg. _____

10. The most popular film in 1997: _____ pg. _____

11. The number of people in the United States who died as a result of a fall in 1996: _____ pg. _____

12. The 1995 winner of the Pulitzer Prize for Criticism: _____ pg. _____

13. The 1999 female champion in United States Figure Skating: _____ pg. _____

14. The 1978 World Cup champion: _____ pg. _____

15. The average price of gasoline fuel in 1960: _____ pg. _____

16. The median family income of Blacks in 1999: _____ pg. _____

17. The popular vote total for William Taft in the 1908 election: _____ pg. _____

18. The median income for men who have…

    a. a bachelor's degree: _____ pg. _____

    b. only a high school diploma: _____ pg. _____

    c. no high school diploma: _____ pg. _____

19. The state song of Texas: _____ pg. _____

20. The world's largest island: _____ pg. _____

Doing Efficient Searches on the Internet

OBJECTIVE

Students will be able to conduct more effective and efficient research on the Internet.

MATERIALS

Overhead or LCD projector
Computer with projector
Instructor's copy of Guide to Google

Overhead
Guide to Google

Worksheets (one per student)
Guide to Google
Independent Practice

Answer Key Overhead
Independent Practice

APPROXIMATE TIME

20 minutes

Introduction

■ **G**ain students' attention.

■ **R**eview key details from the most recent lesson (if applicable).

■ Clearly state the **O**bjective of the lesson:

☐ "In today's lesson, we are going to practice how to do more efficient and effective searches on the Internet, including how to use the Google search engine."

■ Explain **W**hy students should learn the information.

☐ Explain to students that using the Internet for research can be an effective time-saving strategy. Discuss how digital data is only a click away, making it much faster to gather and sort information than paging through reference books and other printed materials. Be sure to mention, however, that online searches can be slow and cumbersome if their topic is too broad or general.

Teacher Input/Modeling

■ Use direct instruction to teach students what words and phrases can be typed into a search engine to produce better research results.

☐ Ask students to raise their hand if they have ever done an online search that took much longer than they expected, or they never found what they needed. (You should see some hands go up.)

☐ Lead a discussion by asking students to share their experiences, including what problems they encountered during their searches that made them more difficult or time consuming.

Guided/Independent Practice

■ Follow up with guided instruction on how to use the Google search engine. Ideally, you will use a computer with a projector to teach the lesson. As you type queries or searches into Google, project your computer screen onto a wall or video screen so students can watch and follow along. If you do not have access to a computer with a projector, use the Guide to Google overhead.

☐ Distribute copies of the Guide to Google worksheet. Teach from the instructor's copy, which includes teacher comments and examples for you and your students to follow. Demonstrate different search strategies and how specific guidelines make searches more efficient.

☐ For active participation, call students up to the computer (if available) and have them type in search words. Periodically ask for feedback and check for understanding.

■ Have students work independently to determine the best search strategies.

☐ Distribute copies of the Independent Practice worksheet. Review the directions with the class, and then instruct students to complete the exercise.

Closure/Review

■ Review students' worksheets using the Independent Practice Answer Key overhead, either at the end of the lesson or the following day. Call on students to share their answers aloud before revealing the answers written on the overhead.

■ To summarize the lesson, verbally quiz the students by asking questions about online searches. Sample questions to ask include:

☐ What do I type in if I only want information from educational Web sites?

☐ How do I find a Web site that is related to one that I have already used?

Connection/Extension

■ The search strategies in this lesson apply to any research activities students do on the Internet. To reinforce the lesson, have students do an online research project.

■ This lesson also serves as a nice transition to discussions about the reliability and validity of information found online.

Guide to Google: Refining Your Internet Searches

WHAT YOU WANT	HOW TO GET IT (type in)	EXAMPLE
To find a certain type of Web site, such as an education site or government agency	Site:edu topic name	You want to find information about missions to Mars on educational Web sites only. Type: Site:edu missions to mars **Teacher comments:** By including "site:" in your query, your search will be restricted to Web sites from that specific domain: "edu" (educational sites), "gov" (government sites), "com" (commercial sites), "mil" (military sites), "net" (networks and organizations), and "org" "(non-profit organizations). When you have a broad topic, it's important to refine your search in some way, otherwise you can end up with thousands or millions of results. Note that there is no space between "site:" and the domain (or following word). **Search result example:** www.aoe.vt.edu/~cdhall/Space/archives/cat_design.html
To see if a particular Web site has information on your topic	Site:Web address topic name	You want to know what information NASA has about missions to Mars. Type: Site:www.nasa.gov mars missions **Teacher comments:** When you want information on a topic to come from a single source, you can specify a Web site so that all of the search results are documents and Web pages from that site. **Search result example:** www.jpl.nasa.gov/
To find a certain type of file, such as a PowerPoint document	Topic name filetype:ppt PowerPoint (.ppt) Rich Text Format (.rtf) Adobe Acrobat PDF (.pdf) Microsoft Word (.doc) Microsoft Excel (.xls) Adobe PostScript (.ps)	You are only interested in finding PowerPoint documents about missions to Mars. Type: Mars missions filetype:ppt **Teacher comments:** If you type the search words "mars mission PowerPoint," your results may include more than just PowerPoint files. However, by typing the phrase "filetype:" followed immediately by the abbreviation of the kind of file you're looking for, your search will bring up only those types of documents. **Search result example:** www.marsinstitute.info/epo/docs/jan05/naderi_intro.ppt

Lesson 25: Instructor Copy

Guide to Google: Refining Your Internet Searches (continued)

WHAT YOU WANT	HOW TO GET IT (type in)	EXAMPLE
To find a Web site that has your topic included in its name or homepage	Allintitle:topic name	You are looking for a Web site that has the phrase "mars missions" as part of its title. Type: allintitle:mars missions **Teacher comments:** Adding the phrase "allintitle:" to your query will give you any documents or Web pages that have your search words in their title. Again, be aware that there is no space between "allintitle:" and whatever word that follows. **Search result example:** marsprogram.jpl.nasa.gov/missions/future/phoenix.html
To find a Web site that has your topic in its "url" address	inurl:topic name	You are looking for a Web site that has "mars missions" in its "url" address. Type: inurl:mars missions **Teacher comments:** Adding the phrase "inurl:" to your query will give you any Web sites or pages that include the topic name (or search words) in their "url" address. Note, however, that there can be no space between the "inurl:" and the following word. **Search result example:** www.themissiontomars.com
To find other Web sites similar to one that you like	Related:Web address	You are looking for other Web sites that are similar to www.nasa.gov. Type: Related:www.nasa.gov **Teacher comments:** Adding the phrase "related:" to your query will give you a list of Web sites that are similar to the one you specified, helping you avoid having to click on countless Web sites that are of little interest to you. Again, do not put any space between "related:" and the word that follows. **Search result example:** www.noaa.gov/

Guide to Google: Refining Your Internet Searches

Name: _____ Date: _____

WHAT YOU WANT	HOW TO GET IT (type in)	EXAMPLE
To find a certain type of Web site, such as an education site or government agency	Site:edu topic name	You want to find information about missions to Mars on educational Web sites only. Type: Site:edu missions to mars
To see if a particular Web site has information on your topic	Site:Web address topic name	You want to know what information NASA has about missions to Mars. Type: Site:www.nasa.gov mars missions
To find a certain type of file, such as a PowerPoint document	Topic name filetype:ppt PowerPoint (.ppt) Rich Text Format (.rtf) Adobe Acrobat PDF (.pdf) Microsoft Word (.doc) Microsoft Excel (.xls) Adobe PostScript (.ps)	You are only interested in finding PowerPoint documents about missions to Mars. Type: Mars missions filetype:ppt
To find a Web site that has your topic included in its name or homepage	Allintitle:topic name	You are looking for a Web site that has the phrase "mars missions" as part of its title.
To find a Web site that has your topic in its "url" address	inurl:topic name	You are looking for a Web site that has "mars missions" in its "url" address. Type: inurl:mars missions
To find other Web sites similar to one that you like	Related:Web address	You are looking for other Web sites that are similar to www.nasa.gov. Type: Related:www.nasa.gov

Independent Practice

Name: _____ Date: _____

Directions: *Read each statement, and then write down the most appropriate search terms (from those discussed in the lesson) for generating relevant results.*

WHAT YOU WANT	HOW TO GET IT
You want to find government statistics on car accidents involving teens.	
You are looking for a job in Omaha, Nebraska. You know that www.omaha.com includes a list of jobs, but you don't want to search through the entire site.	
You are searching for a PowerPoint document on the history of rock 'n' roll.	
You want to find more information on hybrid cars. You think the Web site www. howstuffworks.com has the information you need.	
You have used www.cnn.com as a news source, and you want to find other similar Web sites.	
You are searching for an overview of the Korean War.	
You want to find a Web site similar to www.weather.com.	

Lesson 25: Worksheet

Independent Practice

(answers may vary)

WHAT YOU WANT	HOW TO GET IT
You want to find government statistics on car accidents involving teens.	*site:gov teen car accident stats*
You are looking for a job in Omaha, Nebraska. You know that www.omaha.com includes a list of jobs, but you don't want to search through the entire site.	*site:www.omaha.com jobs*
You are searching for a PowerPoint document on the history of rock 'n' roll.	*history of rock 'n' roll filetype:ppt*
You want to find more information on hybrid cars. You think the Web site www.howstuffworks.com has the information you need.	*site:www.howstuffworks.com hybrid cars*
You have used www.cnn.com as a news source, and you want to find other similar Web sites.	*related:www.cnn.com*
You are searching for an overview of the Korean War.	*several possible answers, including:* a. *site:www.cnn.com Korean War* b. *inurl:Korean War* c. *allintitle:Korean War* d. *site:gov Korean War* e. *site:edu Korean War*
You want to find a Web site similar to www.weather.com.	*related:www.weather.com*

Test-Taking Strategies

In the previous sections, each lesson plan was focused on empowering students to be competent and capable learners – more capable of taking effective notes during lectures and from printed texts; more capable of summarizing information and capturing meaning; and more capable of doing research using appropriate research tools. The overall goal was to give students a stronger foundation and broader perspective for finding success in the classroom. That success, of course, is most often measured and defined by testing.

Unfortunately, tests – standardized, objective, subjective, essay, multiple choice, true/false, and short answer, or any other variation – are a source of great frustration and tension for many students. Studies show that test anxiety can undermine student performance, regardless of age or grade level. In a class of 25, it's estimated that at least five students will perform below expectations due to stress and anxiety.[1] Perfectionists and worriers may be the most at risk for being overwhelmed by nerves, but any student is vulnerable to "test stress."[2] That's why, for some students, doing all the normal things to prepare for an exam isn't always enough and doesn't necessarily guarantee a good score.

In the previous lessons, the basic issue was one of competence. Now, the issue is one of confidence. When students have the skills to organize, synthesize, and research information, preparing for exams doesn't feel so daunting. Yet, when students still feel uncomfortable about taking or while taking a test, it can show in the results. Teaching students to become better test takers is the focus of the next four lesson plans. Students will learn how to answer objective and subjective test questions, take a standardized test, and, perhaps most importantly, manage their stress.

---

[1] Cizek, G.J., & Burg, S.S. (2005). **Addressing test anxiety in a high-stakes environment: Strategies for classrooms and schools.** Thousand Oaks, CA: Corwin Press.

[2] TeensHealth. (2007). Test Anxiety [Online].
Available: http://kidshealth.org/teen/school_jobs/school/test_anxiety.html

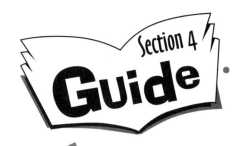

Section 4

Test-Taking Lessons

Understanding and Taking Different Types of Tests

OBJECTIVE

Students will be able to differentiate between various types of tests and use multiple strategies to answer objective and subjective test questions.

MATERIALS

Overhead or LCD projector

Overheads
Types of Tests
Objective Test Strategies:
  Multiple Choice
Objective Test Strategies:
  True or False
Objective Test Strategies:
  Completion/Fill in the Blank
Subjective Test Strategies:
  Short Answer
Subjective Test Strategies:
  Essay

Worksheets (one per student)
Student Notes
Types of Tests Quiz

Answer Key Overhead
Types of Tests

APPROXIMATE TIME

50 minutes or
five 10-minute mini-lessons

Introduction

- **G**ain students' attention.
- **R**eview key details from the most recent lesson (if applicable).
- Clearly state the **O**bjective of the lesson:
  - □ "In today's lesson, we are going to review several different types of tests and test-taking strategies to help you become better test takers."
- Explain **W**hy students should learn the information.
  - □ Reiterate that this lesson can help students become better test takers. Point out that students who spend several hours studying for an exam sometimes will score lower than students who spent less time studying. One reason why this happens is because some students are better test takers. They know how to manage their time, find clues to answers hidden in other test questions, and know when an answer is obviously wrong or right.

Teacher Input/Modeling

- Use direct instruction to teach strategies for answering subjective and objective test questions.
  - □ Using the overheads, go through each of the different types of tests. Have students follow along by filling in the blanks on their Student Notes worksheet (distributed earlier).
  - □ For active participation, have students answer the sample question written on the overhead using the strategies just discussed. If a sample question involves content that is unfamiliar to your students, substitute a more appropriate question. Periodically ask for feedback and check for understanding.

Guided/Independent Practice

■ Test students over the strategies introduced in the lesson.

    □ Tell students that they will have a quiz (the following day or after the last mini-lesson if you divide the lesson into five sessions) on the test-taking strategies they learned. If they don't ask what kind of quiz it will be (true/false, multiple choice, short answer, etc.), prompt them.

    □ Use your discretion as to whether or not students will be allowed to use their notes during the quiz.

Closure/Review

■ At the end of the lesson, have students turn to a partner and give at least two examples of a test-taking strategy for each of the five types of tests.

■ On the day of the quiz, use the Types of Tests Answer Key overhead to review students' quizzes. Ask students to share their answers aloud, before revealing the answers written on the overhead.

■ After the quiz review, discuss their upcoming exams. Ask students which tactics will help them the most, and talk about any other test-taking strategies they use that were not covered in the lesson.

Connection/Extension

■ This lesson can be broken down into five mini-lessons, where each strategy is taught separately. Ideally, you would teach the relevant strategy prior to an exam of that type.

Types of Tests

1. **Objective**
    - **Multiple Choice**
    - **True/False**
    - **Completion or Fill in the Blank**

2. **Subjective**
    - **Short Answer**
    - **Essay**

Objective Test Strategies Multiple Choice

EXAMPLE

The largest state, in terms of area, in the United States is:

A. Canada   B. Rhode Island   C. Alaska   D. Puerto Rico

- **Follow the exam's instructions correctly. Are you asked to circle, underline, fill in the bubble, or do something else?**

- **Eliminate obviously wrong answers.**

- **Look for two answer choices that are opposites; one is likely to be the correct answer.**

- **When you're unsure, see if other test questions reveal clues about the correct answer.**

- **When you're unsure, look for language that comes directly out of the text or from your teacher's lecture.**

- **Do NOT choose "all of the above" if you know at least one of the answer choices is incorrect.**

- **Choose "none of the above" if you're almost certain several of the answer choices are incorrect, and there is no option that includes multiple answers, such as "A and C."**

- **If there is a penalty for leaving questions unanswered, try to answer all of the test questions, even if you have to guess.**

- **Only change your answer when you're 100% certain your first choice was incorrect.**

Objective Test Strategies
True or False

EXAMPLE

Drivers should always stop for a yellow light.   True   False

- **Follow the exam's instructions correctly.**
  Are you asked to circle the "T" or "F," write "True" or "False," or do something else?

- **If ANY part of a statement is false, choose false.**

- **Statements with absolutes are often false.**
  - **always, every, only, never, entirely**

- **Statements with qualifiers are often true.**
  - **usually, often, sometimes, frequently, generally**

- **If there is a penalty for leaving questions unanswered, try to answer all of the test questions, even if you have to guess.**
  - **Longer statements tend to be false.**
  - **Many teachers write tests that have more true than false answers.**
  - **Review past tests to see if there are any patterns.**

Objective Test Strategies Completion/Fill in the Blank

EXAMPLE: ___ geology
___ sociology
___ hematology
___ biology
___ epidemiologist

_1_ is the study of life, while _2_ is the study of the Earth, and _3_ is the study of how humans interact with each other, while an _4_ studies diseases.

- Follow the exam's instructions correctly. Are you asked to circle, underline, fill in the blank, or do something else?

- When the directions don't specify, ask the teacher if any words can be used more than once.

- Watch for clues, such as the word "an" before a word that starts with a vowel sound.

- Answer the easiest questions first, using a process of elimination.

- If there is a penalty for leaving questions unanswered, try to answer all of the test questions, even if you have to guess.

- When you're unsure, see if other test questions reveal clues about the correct answer.

Subjective Test Strategies Short Answer

EXAMPLE
Who is the most deceitful character in the novel,
The Adventures of Huckleberry Finn?

- **Follow the exam's instructions correctly. Are you asked to write your answer using partial sentences (fragments), complete sentences, paragraphs, or something else?**

- **When the directions do not specify, and you cannot ask the teacher, always write your answers in complete sentences.**

- **When answering in complete sentences, start with a sentence that restates key information provided in the question.**

  - Example: The most deceitful character in *The Adventures of Huckleberry Finn* is….

- **When the exam also has objective questions, check to see if any of those questions include details that you can use to support your answer.**

Subjective Test Strategies Essay

EXAMPLE:

Many people criticize the United States for not entering World War II sooner. Do you agree with that criticism? Give at least three specific details to support your answer.

- **Follow the exam's instructions correctly. Are you asked to write in pen, pencil, or something else?**

- **Ask the teacher how many points each essay question is worth, if it's not written on the test.**

- **Answer any objective questions first because they may provide information you can use in your essay.**

- **Manage your time so you can complete the essay question without being rushed.**

- **Be sure to answer everything that is asked in the essay question (some might ask you to compare AND contrast, or write a response that addresses multiple issues).**

Subjective Test Strategies: Essay (continued)

- Use your best writing skills, and start your answer by restating key information provided in the question.

- If time permits, go back and edit your essay to correct any errors or add additional details.

- If time slips away and there's no way you can finish the essay before the exam period ends, outline the details and facts you would have included in your answer. You might earn partial credit from your teacher.

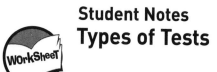

Student Notes
Types of Tests

Name: _____ Date: _____

Types of Tests

1. ## Objective

   ■

   ■ True/False

   ■

2. ## Subjective

   ■

   ■

Objective Test Strategies – Multiple Choice

Name: _____ Date: _____

EXAMPLE: The largest state, in terms of area, in the United States is:
A. Canada
B. Rhode Island
C. Alaska
D. Puerto Rico

- Follow the exam's instructions correctly. Are you asked to circle, underline, fill in the bubble, or do something else?

- Eliminate obviously _____

- _____

- When you're unsure, see if other test questions reveal clues about the correct answer.

- When you're unsure, look for language that comes directly out of the text or from your teacher's lecture.

- _____ "all of the above" if you know at least one of the answer choices is incorrect.

- Choose "none of the above" if you're almost certain several of the answer choices are incorrect, and there is no option that includes multiple answers, such as "A and C."

- If there is a penalty for leaving questions unanswered, try to answer all of the test questions, even if you have to guess.

- Only change your answer when you're 100% certain your first choice was incorrect.

Objective Test Strategies – True or False

Name: _____ Date: _____

EXAMPLE:

Drivers should always stop for a yellow light.   True False

- Follow the exam's instructions correctly. Are you asked to circle the "T" or "F," write "True" or "False," or do something else?

- If **ANY** part of a statement is false, choose _____.

- Statements with **absolutes** are often **false**.

  ☐

- Statements with **qualifiers** are often **true**.

  ☐

- If there is a penalty for leaving questions unanswered, try to answer all of the test questions, even if you have to guess.

  ☐

  ☐ Many teachers write tests that have more true than false answers.

  ☐

Objective Test Strategies – Completion/Fill in the Blank

Name: _____ Date: _____

EXAMPLE:
    ___ geology
    ___ sociology
    ___ hematology
    ___ biology
    ___ epidemiologist

     1 is the study of life, while 2 is the study of the Earth, and 3 is the study of how humans interact with each other, while an 4 studies diseases.

- Follow the exam's instructions correctly. Are you asked to circle, underline, fill in the blank, or do something else?

-

- Watch for clues, such as the word "an" before a word that starts with a vowel sound.

-

- If there is a penalty for leaving questions unanswered, try to answer all of the test questions, even if you have to guess.

- When you're unsure, see if other test questions reveal clues about the correct answer.

Subjective Test Strategies – Short Answer

Name: _____   Date: _____

EXAMPLE:

Who is the most deceitful character in the novel, *The Adventures of Huckleberry Finn*?

- Follow the exam's instructions correctly. Are you asked to write your answer using partial sentences (fragments), complete sentences, paragraphs, or something else?

-

- When answering in complete sentences, start with a sentence that _____
  _____.

  - Example: The most deceitful character in *The Adventures of Huckleberry Finn* is....

- When the exam also has objective questions, check to see if any of those questions include details that you can use to support your answer.

Subjective Test Strategies – Essay

Name: _____ Date: _____

EXAMPLE:

Many people criticize the United States for not entering World War II sooner. Do you agree with that criticism? Give at least three specific details to support your answer.

- Follow the exam's instructions correctly. Are you asked to write in pen, pencil, or something else?

-

-

- Manage your time so you can complete the essay question without being rushed.

-

- Use your best writing skills, and start your answer by restating key information provided in the question.

-

- If time slips away and there's no way you can finish the essay before the exam period ends, outline the details and facts you would have included in your answer. You might earn partial credit from your teacher.

Types of Tests – Quiz

Name: _____ Date: _____

Directions: *Take out a sheet of paper to record your answers to the following questions. You have 15 minutes to complete the quiz.*

Multiple Choice: Write the capital letter of the correct answer on your paper. *(1 point each)*

1. Which of the following are good strategies to apply on a multiple-choice test:
   A. Never guess
   B. Eliminate obviously wrong answers
   C. Both of the above
   D. None of the above

2. Which of the following are "absolutes" in true/false statements:
   A. Every
   B. Only
   C. Never
   D. All of the above

3. Which of the following is a clue on a completion-type of test:
   A. A false statement is usually longer
   B. The word "an" before a blank signals a word beginning in a vowel sound
   C. Start with a complete sentence
   D. Never guess

4. Which of the following would be the best way to begin an answer to the essay question: Why is Condoleezza Rice an important woman in American history?
   A. Because she has been Secretary of State and National Security Advisor…
   B. She is the first African-American to serve as National Security Advisor…
   C. No one knows much about her
   D. Condoleezza Rice is an important woman in American history because…

True/False: Record your answer using a "+" for true statements and a "0" for false statements.
(1 point each)

_____ 1. On multiple-choice tests, you should only change an answer if you're 100% certain that your first choice was incorrect.

_____ 2. On true/false tests, statements with qualifiers are often true.

_____ 3. On true/false tests, longer statements tend to be true.

_____ 4. Some teachers create a pattern of true/false answers on tests.

_____ 5. On completion tests, you should do the easiest questions first.

_____ 6. On short answer tests, if the directions don't specify, you can begin with an incomplete sentence.

Short Answer: Use your best writing skills to answer the following question. (5 points)

What are three strategies that can help you do better on an essay test?

_____

_____

_____

_____

_____

_____

_____

_____

_____

_____

_____

_____

Types of Tests

Multiple Choice: Write the capital letter of the correct answer on your paper. *(1 point each)*

1. Which of the following are good strategies to apply on a multiple-choice test:
   B. Eliminate obviously wrong answers
2. Which of the following are "absolutes" in true/false statements:
   D. All of the above
3. Which of the following is a clue on a completion-type of test:
   B. The word "an" before a blank signals a word beginning in a vowel sound
4. Which of the following would be the best way to begin an answer to the essay question: Why is Condoleezza Rice an important woman in American history?
   D. Condoleezza Rice is an important woman in American history because…

True/False: Record your answer using a "+" for true statements and a "0" for false statements. *(1 point each)*

__+__ 1. On multiple-choice tests, you should only change an answer if you're 100% certain that your first choice was incorrect.

__+__ 2. On true/false tests, statements with qualifiers are often true.

__0__ 3. On true/false tests, longer statements tend to be true.

__+__ 4. Some teachers create a pattern of true/false answers on tests.

__+__ 5. On completion tests, you should do the easiest questions first.

__0__ 6. On short answer tests, if the directions don't specify, you can begin with an incomplete sentence.

Short Answer: Use your best writing skills to answer the following question. (5 points)

What are three strategies that can help you do better on an essay test?

I can do better on an essay test if I manage my time so I won't be rushed. I also can edit my essay to correct any errors or add details, if I have time to do that. And finally, I can do what I did in this answer, which is to begin by restating the question.

* Responses to the short answer question will vary. However, the first sentence should restate key words from the question.

LESSON **27**

Preparing for Standardized Tests

OBJECTIVE

Students will be able to use practical strategies to prepare for and take standardized tests, including identifying the strategies that are best suited for them.

MATERIALS

Overhead or LCD projector

Overhead
ABC's of Test Taking

Worksheets (one per student)
ABC's of Test Taking
Standardized Test Example

Answer Key Overhead
Standardized Test Example

APPROXIMATE TIME

40 minutes

Introduction

- **G**ain students' attention.
- **R**eview key details from the most recent lesson (if applicable).
- Clearly state the **O**bjective of the lesson:
  - □ "In today's lesson, we are going to review several strategies that can help you better prepare for standardized tests, and then practice using those strategies by taking a timed quiz."
- Explain **W**hy students should learn the information.
  - □ Explain to students that standardized tests are part of academic life and that many of them probably have taken more than one. Point out that most exams that require students to fill in an oval or bubble in order to answer the questions are standardized. Define "standardized test" as an exam that is administered and graded the same way, regardless of who is being tested or where. The test results can be compared to others who are similar to them, in terms of geographic region, age, or grade level.

Teacher Input/Modeling

- Use direct instruction to introduce the ABC's of test taking.
  - □ Prior to the lesson, jot down on the board or an overhead, several examples of standardized tests. You could include the ACT, ITBS, CAT, and ASVAB exams. Ask students which ones, if any, they have taken or know about. Start a discussion about why such tests are used. Prompt students by providing an example, such as:

      A guidance counselor might look at the results of a standardized test before recommending whether or not a student should take an elective class.

Employers sometimes require all job applicants to take a standardized exam to measure their qualifications for a job.

The military uses results from standardized tests to encourage students or new recruits to pursue certain career paths.

Local and state governments use standardized tests and their results to compare schools and determine which ones are "successful" or "underperforming."

- Follow up with guided instruction. Use the ABC's of Test Taking overhead to introduce eleven test-taking strategies.

  □ Have students follow along by filling in the corresponding worksheet (distributed earlier). Add any additional comments or guidelines you deem necessary. For active participation, have students circle two strategies that they have not used but think will help them perform better on standardized tests. Call on students to share their selections and explain their reasoning.

Guided/Independent Practice

- Use a timed quiz to test students' understanding of the strategies discussed.

  □ Distribute copies of the Standardized Test Example worksheet. Review the instructions with the class, modeling what you would do prior to administering a real standardized exam. Permit students to use their notes so the strategies are reinforced.

  □ After reviewing the instructions, set a timer for five minutes and tell the class to begin. At the halfway mark, announce the time. Give a second time warning at the one-minute mark. When time expires, tell students to stop.

  □ The sample quiz is designed so that students, including the fastest readers, will be rushed to finish. This is intended to reinforce the "G" strategy (guessing when appropriate and necessary).

Closure/Review

- Use the Standardized Test Example Answer Key overhead to review students' quizzes. Ask students to share their answers aloud, before revealing the answers written on the overhead.

- Lead a class discussion about which test-taking strategies seemed the most useful during the timed quiz. Remind students that just one or two correct guesses on an exam, such as the ACT, can raise a score by an entire point. Encourage students to use the strategies, when appropriate, before and during their next standardized exam.

Connection/Extension

- If students need additional practice using the ABC's of test taking, give another timed quiz using a reading passage and questions from an actual standardized exam.

- This lesson can be used as a pre-teaching activity prior to scheduled exams, such as the Iowa Tests of Basic Skills or other similar standardized testing. This lesson can also be tied to a discussion about how best to prepare for and take regular classroom exams and quizzes.

The ABC's of Test-Taking

Arrive early.
- 10 - 15 minutes
- too soon, you may get bored, tired, or overly anxious
- too late, you may feel rushed and waste valuable energy to stress and worry

Be prepared.
- What materials are required?
  - ☐ The ACT requires a registration card, #2 pencils, and an approved calculator
- If you are allowed the use of a calculator, but didn't bring one, you have given the other test takers an advantage over you

Change an answer only if you're 100% certain it is incorrect.
- Trust your gut; many times changing an answer results in an incorrect response

Do the easy questions first.
- Builds confidence
- May give you answers or hints to some of the more difficult questions

Eat an appropriate meal.
- Should contain a carbohydrate and a protein
  - ☐ Examples: toast and peanut butter, breakfast burrito, meat pizza

Follow all directions.
- Verbal: If the ACT test proctor (room supervisor) sees you open your book early, you will be asked to leave
- Written: If the directions say to "print," make sure you do not write in cursive

The ABC's of Test-Taking (continued)

Guess (if you will lose points for leaving questions unanswered, try to answer all questions).

Increase your chances by eliminating obviously wrong answers.
- By crossing out one of four answers, you improve your odds from 25% to 33%
- Eliminate two wrong answers, and your odds become 50-50

Never allow yourself to sleep between tests (if taking more than one test back-to-back).
- Slows your brain down
- May take you several minutes into the next exam before you are "geared back up"

Stay consistent if time is running out and several questions remain unanswered.
- Applies only to situations in which time is critically short, and unanswered questions will cause you to lose points
- Stick with all B or C answers the rest of the way down your answer sheet
- **CAUTION:** Only follow this tip when absolutely necessary

Use your time wisely.
- If you finish early, go back and double check your answers – especially the ones which were more difficult
- Wear a watch, and know when time is half over, five minutes remain, and one minute remains

The ABC's of Test Taking

Name: _____ Date: _____

Arrive early.
- ■ 10 - 15 minutes
- ■ too soon, you may get bored, tired, or overly anxious
- ■ too late, you may feel rushed and waste valuable energy to stress and worry

B
- ■
- ■

C
- ■

Do the easy questions first.
- ■
- ■

E
- ■

F
- ■
- ■

Guess.

I
- ■
- ■

N
- ■
- ■

S
- ■
- ■
- ■

Use your time wisely.
- ■
- ■

Lesson 27: Worksheet

Name: _____ Date: _____

5 Minutes - 10 Questions

Directions: *After reading the following passage, choose the best answer to each question and fill in the corresponding oval at the bottom of each page. You may refer to the passage and your notes as often as needed. You have five minutes to complete the exam.*

Line 1   *Forbes* magazine and its companion Internet Web site, Forbes.com, are known for their lists. Among these is the Forbes Celebrity Top 100. Compiling the list was not just a matter of picking favorites. Editors attempted to make the concept of celebrity tangible by rating famous

Line 5   people in 14 different categories, including earnings, Web site hits, press clips, and magazine covers. They totaled up the scores and gave each celebrity a power ranking. Tops on the list for 2001 was Tom Cruise. Although he was only thirteenth in earnings, his combined scores for the other categories made him the most powerful celebrity in the country.

Line 10   Rounding out the top ten were Tiger Woods, the Beatles, Britney Spears, Bruce Willis, Michael Jordan, the Backstreet Boys, 'N Sync, Oprah Winfrey, and Mel Gibson. Although Oprah sat at ninth place in the power rankings, she was second in earnings, with $150 million to her credit. First place in earnings went to George Lucas, cashing in at $250 million.

Line 15   All of the people on this list enjoyed the popularity, wealth, and fame of being a celebrity. Most are easily identifiable because the American public is constantly bombarded with their images and news of their activities on television, in magazines and newspapers, and on movie screens. America's infatuation with celebrities has become a multi-billion dollar industry. But

Line 20   let us resolve never to look upon celebrities as role models or heroes, and never to blur the line between those who are merely famous and those who make a real sacrifice in the name of duty and service.

    Celebrities do not risk their lives every day as part of their jobs. Police officers, firefighters, servicemen and servicewomen, and countless

Line 25   others who keep us safe and secure do. By definition, these people are the

Line 26   real heroes who deserve our respect and admiration.

1. As it is used in this passage, the word *tangible* (line 4) most nearly means:
   A. understandable.
   B. physically present.
   C. confusing.
   D. totally obsolete.

2. The main focus of the passage's opening paragraph is:
   A. to introduce Tom Cruise.
   B. to garner interest in the Forbes.com Web site.
   C. to define the term "celebrity."
   D. to introduce the Top 100 celebrities.

3. The passage states that:
   A. Oprah was higher in the earnings category than she was in the power rankings.
   B. George Lucas held first place in power rankings and earnings.
   C. Tiger Woods was the most powerful celebrity for that year.
   D. the Backstreet Boys and 'N Sync were tied in the overall combined scores.

4. The passage implies that:
   A. celebrities have earned their status and, thus, deserve to be well paid for their contributions.
   B. newspapers, magazines, television, and movies have a huge impact on whom Americans recognize.
   C. Americans would be wise to invest in Forbes.com and other media that identify famous people.
   D. people from other countries desire to have the same celebrity status as popular Americans.

5. As it is used in this passage, the word *resolve* (line 20) most nearly means:
   A. to work out differences.
   B. to make a commitment to do.
   C. to offer money for services.
   D. to be willing to do.

1. ○ A	2. ○ A	3. ○ A	4. ○ A	5. ○ A
○ B	○ B	○ B	○ B	○ B
○ C	○ C	○ C	○ C	○ C
○ D	○ D	○ D	○ D	○ D

6. The passage states that:
    A. Americans spend more on celebrities than they do on food.
    B. America's infatuation with celebrities is a multi-billion dollar industry.
    C. celebrities earn more than any other profession in the United States.
    D. celebrities make a lot of money, but they aren't very happy people.

7. The information in lines 20-21 suggests that celebrities:
    A. make real sacrifices for our country.
    B. and heroes are basically the same thing.
    C. should not be considered heroes.
    D. are famous because of their duty and service to our country.

8. As it is used in this passage, the word *sacrifice* (line 21) most nearly means:
    A. something offered to appease the gods.
    B. something abandoned in a time of need.
    C. something given up for the sake of others.
    D. something important to being famous.

9. In line 23 of the passage, "every day":
    A. is written correctly as two words.
    B. should be written as one word.
    C. should be hyphenated.
    D. should be taken out altogether.

10. The best title for this passage would be:
    A. "Heroes Versus Celebrities"
    B. "Celebrities Deserve Respect"
    C. "Making Millions"
    D. "Forbes.com"

6. ○ A	7. ○ A	8. ○ A	9. ○ A	10. ○ A
○ B	○ B	○ B	○ B	○ B
○ C	○ C	○ C	○ C	○ C
○ D	○ D	○ D	○ D	○ D

Standardized Test Example

1. *A   understandable*

2. *C   to define the term "celebrity"*

3. *A   Oprah was higher in the earnings category than she
   was in the power rankings*

4. *B   newspapers, magazines, television, and movies have a
   huge impact on whom Americans recognize*

5. *B   to make a commitment to do*

6. *B   America's infatuation with celebrities is a multi-billion
   dollar industry*

7. *C   should not be considered heroes*

8. *C   something given up for the sake of others*

9. *A   is written correctly as two words*

10. *A   "Heroes Versus Celebrities"*

Recognizing and Responding to Different Question Categories

OBJECTIVE

Students will be able to categorize questions using the question-answer-relationship (QAR) strategy to improve their reading comprehension skills.

MATERIALS

Overhead or LCD projector

Overheads
Four Categories of Questions
Right There Questions
Think and Search Questions
Author and Me Questions
On My Own Questions

Worksheets (one per student)
Four Categories of Questions
Questions and Categories

Answer Key Overhead
Questions and Categories

APPROXIMATE TIME

20 minutes

Introduction

- **G**ain students' attention.
- **R**eview key details from the most recent lesson (if applicable).
- Clearly state the **O**bjective of the lesson:
  - □ "In today's lesson, we are going to practice using the QAR strategy to search for answers in printed text based on the type of question being asked."
- Explain **W**hy students should learn the information.
  - □ Explain to students that when they understand the type of question being asked, they can organize their thoughts and strategically search for the right answer. This skill can help them perform better on assignments and tests.

Teacher Input/Modeling

- Use direct instruction to define and explain the question-answer-relationship (QAR) strategy. (QAR is a reading comprehension strategy designed to help students recognize four different types of questions that they are commonly asked to answer after reading a given text.)
  - □ Call on students to describe the different kinds of questions that they see on tests and assignments. (Offer an example if students are unsure, such as true/false, multiple choice, fill in the blank, short answer, or essay). Discuss how each of these questions requires different responses.
- Follow up with guided instruction. Use the Four Categories of Questions overhead to introduce the four types of questions – Right There, Think and Search, Author and Me, and On My Own.
  - □ One at a time, define and explain each category using its corresponding overhead. Point out that each

category name signifies where, or if, an answer can be found in a given text and how students should approach answering the question. Have students follow along by taking notes on their Four Categories of Questions worksheet (distributed earlier). For active participation, solicit feedback and check for understanding.

Guided/Independent Practice

■ Have students work independently to categorize questions, and then explain how they would approach answering each question based on its category.

   □ Distribute copies of the Questions and Categories worksheet. Review the directions with the class, and then instruct students to complete the exercise.

Closure/Review

■ Use the Questions and Categories Answer Key overhead to review students' worksheets, either at the end of the lesson or the following day. Ask students to share their answers aloud, before revealing the answers written on the overhead.

■ To end the lesson, have students turn to a partner and recall at least two examples of signal words for each of the four types of questions. Call on several students to share their examples aloud.

Connection/Extension

■ This lesson complements any activity in which students will be tested on their reading comprehension skills. You also can use QAR as a pre-teaching opportunity to focus students' attention on specific content prior to a reading assignment.

Four Categories of Questions

Types of Questions

Right There	Author and Me
Think and Search	On My Own

Right There Questions

Signal words:

define, identify, recall, locate, Who?
What? When? Where?

Example:

Who invented the light bulb?

Define homestead.

To answer:

The answer is in the text.

Scan the text until you find the answer.

Think and Search Questions

Signal words:

summarize, give examples, describe, explain, list, cause and effect

Example:

Summarize the life and accomplishments of Babe Ruth.

List and describe three types of venomous snakes.

To answer:

The answer is in the text, however, you may have to scan several sentences, paragraphs, or pages to find the answer. Or, read more than one text.

You may want to take notes to organize your answer.

Author and Me Questions

Signal words:

analyze, predict, compare, contrast, reflect, infer, explain why, draw conclusions

Example:

Predict what you think will happen next in the story, and explain why.

To answer:

The answer is based on your thoughts and knowledge, in addition to information in the text.

You may want to take notes first, and then add your own thoughts.

On My Own Questions

Signal words:

give your opinion, brainstorm, use prior knowledge, make judgments

Example:

What did you enjoy most about the book *The Outsiders*?

To answer:

The answer is based on your thoughts and knowledge. If you have prior knowledge on a topic, you won't need to do any further reading to answer the question.

Four Categories of Questions

Name: _____ Date: _____

Types of Questions

Right There	Author and Me
Signal words: Example: Who invented the light bulb? Define homestead. To answer:	Signal words: Example: Predict what you think will happen next in the story and explain why. To answer:
Think and Search	**On My Own**
Signal words: Example: Summarize the life and accomplishments of Babe Ruth. List and describe three types of venomous snakes. To answer:	Signal words: Example: What did you enjoy most about the book *The Outsiders*? To answer:

Questions and Categories

Name: _____ Date: _____

Directions: *Read each question, then label what category the question falls under and how you would approach finding the answer.*

Types of questions: **Right There, Think and Search, Author and Me** and **On My Own**

QUESTION	QUESTION TYPE	HOW TO ANSWER
1. Compare and contrast insects and spiders.		
2. List the steps of the scientific method.		
3. Write a definition for the word "revolution."		
4. Predict what will happen to Ponyboy.		
5. What is your favorite season, and explain why.		
6. Explain what happened when gold was discovered in California.		
7. Based on the author's description of new inventions, predict which invention will have the biggest impact on American life.		
8. Who was the first man to walk on the moon?		
9. Describe the plot of the story.		
10. Explain the roles of the three branches of the United States government.		
11. If you were president, what would be the first thing that you would do?		
12. Brainstorm a list of things you could do to reduce pollution.		

Questions and Categories

QUESTION	QUESTION TYPE	HOW TO ANSWER
1. Compare and contrast insects and spiders.	*Author and Me*	*text, notes, own thoughts*
2. List the steps of the scientific method.	*Right There*	*text*
3. Write a definition for the word "revolution."	*Right There*	*text*
4. Predict what will happen to Ponyboy.	*Author and Me*	*text, own thoughts*
5. What is your favorite season, and explain why.	*On My Own*	*prior knowledge, own thoughts*
6. Explain what happened when gold was discovered in California.	*Think and Search*	*scan throughout the text*
7. Based on the author's description of new inventions, predict which invention will have the biggest impact on American life.	*Author and Me*	*text, notes, own thoughts*
8. Who was the first man to walk on the moon?	*Right There*	*text*
9. Describe the plot of the story.	*Think and Search*	*scan throughout the text*
10. Explain the roles of the three branches of the United States government.	*Think and Search*	*scan throughout the text*
11. If you were president, what would be the first thing that you would do?	*On My Own*	*prior knowledge, own thoughts*
12. Brainstorm a list of things you could do to reduce pollution.	*On My Own*	*prior knowledge, own thoughts*

Lesson 28: Answer Key Overhead

Overcoming Test Anxiety

OBJECTIVE

Students will be able to identify strategies for managing their anxiety level before and during exams.

MATERIALS

Overhead or LCD projector

Overheads

Overcoming Test Anxiety: Preparing for the Test
Overcoming Test Anxiety: Before Starting the Test
Overcoming Test Anxiety: During the Test
After the Test

Worksheet (one per student)

Overcoming Test Anxiety

APPROXIMATE TIME

20 minutes

Introduction

- **G**ain students' attention.
- **R**eview key details from the most recent lesson (if applicable).
- Clearly state the **O**bjective of the lesson:
  - ☐ "In today's lesson, we are going to review strategies that can help you better manage the stress and anxiety you feel before and during exams."
- Explain **W**hy students should learn the information.
  - ☐ Explain to students that test anxiety is very natural and common, and that a little anxiety can actually be a good thing because it's a sign that they care and want to do their best. Point out, however, that if they let their nerves get the better of them by becoming too tense, they can suffer mental blocks or become so distracted they can't perform up to their ability.

Teacher Input/Modeling

- Use direct instruction to introduce strategies for overcoming test anxiety.
  - ☐ Ask students to raise their hands if they have ever gotten nervous before an exam. (You should see most hands go up.) Point out that their nervousness is a type of test anxiety.
  - ☐ Start a discussion by asking students to share any experiences or moments when they've been really nervous, and how it affected their behavior. Feel free to share your own test-anxiety experiences.
- Follow up with guided instruction on how to manage test anxiety.
  - ☐ Use the Overcoming Test Anxiety overheads to explain basic strategies for coping with stress. Have students

follow along by taking notes on their Overcoming Test Anxiety worksheet (distributed earlier). For active participation, periodically ask for feedback and check for understanding.

Guided/Independent Practice

■ Have students work in groups to discuss each of the strategies.

☐ Ask students to review their notes, and then in their groups discuss which strategies they feel would be most helpful to them. Call on groups to share which strategies they chose and why.

Closure/Review

■ At the end of the lesson, have students turn to a partner and describe at least three strategies to manage anxiety before and during an exam. You also can have students write two additional examples of positive affirmations.

■ Remind students that all of the strategies are helpful, and they should use as many as they can when preparing for and taking tests.

Connection/Extension

■ This lesson provides a nice wrap up to all of the test-taking strategies in this section. You also can connect this lesson to life outside the classroom by pointing out how students have to take driving and employment exams. You might even discuss the different professions that require individuals to pass periodic or annual exams.

OVERCOMING TEST ANXIETY
Preparing for the Test...

- Ask the teacher to explain the test's format (essay, true/false, multiple choice, etc.) so you can use the most appropriate study strategies. Find out if there will be a time limit.

- Study.
  - □ You will be overly anxious if you have not done your part and prepared!

- Get a good night's sleep.

- Think of positive affirmations, and repeat them aloud.
  - □ Your brain is wired to listen to your voice, so say positive affirmations OUT LOUD.
    - "I am going to do well on this test."
    - "I'm going to ace this test."
    - "I am a good student, and I can do well."

- Eat a light, nutritious meal that includes a carbohydrate and a protein.
  - □ Peanut butter and toast
  - □ Regular-sized hamburger

OVERCOMING TEST ANXIETY
Before Starting the Test...

- Walk quickly to the test room.
    - You can burn some nervous energy, and get your mental system "fired up."

- Close your eyes and take a few deep, cleansing breaths.

- Say to yourself one or more positive affirmations.

- Stretch your arms and bend your neck to loosen up.

OVERCOMING TEST ANXIETY
During the Test...

- Jot down any memory aids you prepared.

    - A math formula that is difficult to remember, such as the area of a triangle is 1/2bh.

    - The mnemonic HOMES to recall the names of the five Great Lakes.

- Stay calm and relaxed by taking slow, deep breaths.

- Ease into the exam by answering the easiest questions first.

- Ignore others who finish before you. Concentrate on your work.

Lesson 29: Overhead
©2008, Father Flanagan's Boys' Home

277

After the Test...

- **Don't dwell on the exam, or how you think you did.**

- **After the test is graded and returned, review your answers and any teacher comments. Use that information to prepare for the next exam given by that teacher.**

- **If you think the teacher made a mistake when grading your exam, use a pleasant voice to disagree appropriately.**

  - ☐ **See the teacher privately.**

  - ☐ **Politely ask the teacher to go over the disputed question(s) with you.**

    - **"Mr. Doe, I know you spent a lot of time grading these tests, but would you please explain to me why my answer to this question is wrong?"**

Overcoming Test Anxiety

Name: _____ Date: _____

Preparing for the test...

■ Ask the teacher to explain the test's format (essay, true/false, multiple choice, etc.) so you can use the most appropriate study strategies. Find out if there will be a time limit.

■ _____

  ☐ _____

■ _____

■ Think of positive affirmations, and repeat them aloud.

  ☐ Your brain is wired to listen to your voice, so say positive affirmations OUT LOUD.

    ■ _____

    ■ _____

    ■ _____

■ Eat a light, nutritious meal that includes a carbohydrate and a protein.

  ☐ _____

  ☐ _____

Before starting the test...

■ Walk quickly to the test room.

  ☐ _____

■ Close your eyes and take a few deep, cleansing breaths.

■ _____

■ Stretch your arms and bend your neck to loosen up.

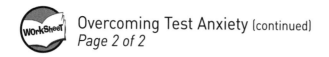

During the test...

- Jot down any memory aids you prepared.

    ☐ _____

    ☐ _____

- Stay calm and relaxed by _____.

- Ease into the exam by answering the easiest questions first.

- _____

After the test...

- _____

- After the test is graded and returned, review your answers and any teacher comments. Use that information to prepare for the next exam given by that teacher.

- If you think the teacher made a mistake when grading your exam, use a pleasant voice to disagree appropriately.

    ☐ _____

    ☐ _____

        ■ _____

Credits

Editor:	Stan Graeve
Cover design:	Eli Hernandez
Page layout:	Anne Hughes
Proofreader:	Terry Hyland
Research assistant:	Betty Ackerson